Alpheus S. Packard, United States Entomological Commission

The Systematic Position of the Orthoptera

in relation to other orders of insects

Alpheus S. Packard, United States Entomological Commission

The Systematic Position of the Orthoptera
in relation to other orders of insects

ISBN/EAN: 9783337311155

Printed in Europe, USA, Canada, Australia, Japan

Cover: Foto ©Andreas Hilbeck / pixelio.de

More available books at **www.hansebooks.com**

THE

SYSTEMATIC POSITION

OF THE

ORTHOPTERA

IN RELATION TO

OTHER ORDERS OF INSECTS.

BY

A. S. PACKARD, Jr., M. D.

[Extracted from the Third Report of the United States Entomological Commission.]

1883.

AUTHOR'S EDITION

THE

SYSTEMATIC POSITION

OF THE

ORTHOPTERA

IN RELATION TO

OTHER ORDERS OF INSECTS.

BY

A. S. PACKARD, Jr., M. D.

[Extracted from the Third Report of the United States Entomological Commission.]

1883.

fourth (labial) segment is quite separate from the rest of the head.
Fig. 11 (in text), copied from our Memoir, also
shows in a saw fly larva (*Nematus ventricosus*) the
relations of the labial or fourth segment to the
rest of the head. The suture between the labial
segment and the pre-oral part of the head disap-
pears in adult life. From this sketch it would
seem that the back part of the head, *i. e.*, of the
epicranium, may be made up in part of the tergite
or pleurites of the mandibular segment, since the
mandibular muscles are inserted on the roof of the
head behind the eyes. It is this segment which
in Corydalis evidently forms the occiput, and of
which in most other insects there is no trace in
larval or adult life.

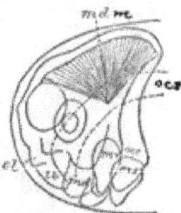

Fig. 11.—Head of embryo
Nematus, showing the labial
segment, *occ*, forming the occiput; *cl*, clypeus; *lb*, labrum;
md, mandible; *mdm*, muscle of
same; *mx*, maxilla; *mx'*, 2d
maxilla (labium); *oes*, oesopha-
gus.

It appears, then, that the epicranium, or that piece (sclerite) bearing
the eyes, ocelli, and antennæ, and in front the clypeus and labrum, is
formed from the original procephalic lobes, and represents the first or
antennal segment, and is pleural, the clypeus and labrum being the tergal portion of the segment; while the remainder of the original or primitive segments are obsolete, except in those insects which retain traces
of an occiput or fourth cephalic tergite. All of the gular region of the
head probably represents the base of the primitive second maxillæ.

CHAPTER XI.

It may not be out of place, considering the amount of space given in
the reports of the Commission to matters of a practical nature, and also
taking into account the fact that these reports are widely sent to entomologists, as well as to farmers and planters, to give the scientific reader
a brief sketch or abstract of the results of an examination of the external anatomy of the Orthoptera in general, of which the locust is a
type. This we have attempted to do, but in undertaking this task we
have been led perforce to examine those insects allied to the Orthoptera, i. e., the Pseudoneuroptera and Neuroptera. This has led us to
review the characteristics of the four lowest orders of winged insects.
The results of this review we here present for the consideration of zool-
ogists. It is believed that so detailed a survey of the external anatomy,
especially of the thorax, of so many forms has not been made before,
although much more thorough and exhaustive studies on a few insects
have been made by Audouin, MacLeay, Newport, Strauss-Durckheim,
Hammond, and others. The results have led us to quite different con-
clusions respecting the classification of the Neuroptera and Orthoptera,
as originally limited by Linnæus, from those which we have heretofore
held. Our work is based on the researches of Audouin, MacLeay, and
Newport, and the terms here used will be found explained in their original works, as well as in the author's "Guide to the Study of Insects."
The reader is also referred to our account of the external anatomy of
the locust in the Second Report of this Commission.

Any one who has examined a cockroach and a white ant, and seen
how closely they resemble each other, must have felt that so far from
representing two distinct orders, they appear rather to be types of two
allied families of the same order. Again, while the larval cockroach
or larval Forficula closely resemble the Thysanurous Lepisma, on the
other hand a larval Perla also nearly approximates to a Lepisma. The
explanation of these facts is to be sought in the probable genealogical
history of the Orthoptera, which, with the Pseudoneuroptera and Dermatoptera, are evidently descendants from an ancestral form like Lepisma, their larvæ closely resembling this Thysanuran. We have therefore indicated in this chapter the probable lines of descent from the
primitive hypothetical Thysanuran.

In making these studies we have, in order to be unbiased, disre-
garded the works of others, and gone over the field anew, as if nothing

286

had been done upon this subject. We have examined the fundamental characters of the head, thorax, and abdomen, points neglected by most systematic writers, not spending much time on the peripheral, *i. e.*, the superficial adaptive characters of the mouth-parts, wings, and legs, which have been elaborated by systematic entomologists; believing that by this method perhaps more thorough and better grounded views might result. The outcome has been to lead us to separate the Neuroptera, as defined farther on, from the Pseudoneuroptera, and to regard these two groups, with the Orthoptera and Dermatoptera, as four orders of a category which may be regarded as a superorder, for which the name *Phyloptera* is proposed, as these four orders are probably closely allied to, if not in some cases identical with, the stem or ancestral groups from which probably all the higher orders—the Hemiptera, Coleoptera, Diptera, Lepidoptera, and Hymenoptera—have originated.

We will first briefly summarize the characters as we understand them of the *Phyloptera* as a whole; then the distinguishing marks of the four orders, then briefly discuss their probable genealogy, closing with a more extended though very condensed account of the essential peculiarities of structure of the families, as represented by one or more of the typical genera.

Superorder PHYLOPTERA.[137]

The mouth-parts are free, adapted invariably for biting; the mandibles being toothed and adapted for chewing; the first maxillæ separate, with three divisions, the outer bearing usually five-jointed palpi; the second maxillæ united to form a labium, divided into a submentum, mentum, and ligula, the latter varying much, being either cleft (Pseudoneuroptera) or entire (Neuroptera), and bearing usually a three-jointed palpus. This is the primitive, elementary condition of the mouth-parts, and such as obtains in Coleopterous larvæ. The head is notable from the great development of the epicranium. The clypeus is often divided into two portions, a posterior (post-clypeus) and anterior (ante-clypeus); in the other and higher orders the clypeus is entire.

The prothorax is usually very large and square, but in a few families, as the Phryganeidæ, Panorpidæ, Psocidæ, Libellulidæ, and Ephemeridæ, it is small and collar-like. There is a marked equality in size and form of the meso- and metathorax; in most Orthoptera and some Pseudoneuroptera and Neuroptera the metathorax is often even larger than the mesothorax; in this respect the *Phyloptera* differ from any of the higher Hexapoda. In both of the two hinder segments of the thorax the four tergal sclerites, viz: the præscutum, scutum, scutellum, and post-scutellum, are each well developed, and more equably so than in the higher orders. The scutum is deeply excavated in front to receive the often large subtriangular or cordate præscutum; and in some genera

---

[137] From φῦλον, gens, nation; πτερόν, wing.

the scutum is, so to speak, cleft in two by the meeting of the præscutum and scutellum in the median line. The flanks of the thorax, or pleurites, are often very large, and the episternum and epimerum are broad, oblong, or squarish, and these sclerites are sometimes subdivided into an upper and lower division (supra- and infra- epinerum or episternum). The sternum is often large, flat, and broad; it is sometimes divided into a sternum and præsternum.

The wings are usually net-veined, often with numerous longitudinal veins, the branches of the subcostal, median, and submedian veins being either very long and parallel with the longitudinal axis of the wing, or numerous and small (especially in the hind wings of Orthoptera).

The hind wings are often (Orthoptera and O. onata) broader and larger than the anterior pair, the metathorax in such cases being a little larger than the mesothorax.

The abdomen has in this group, including representatives of the Neuroptera, Orthoptera, Dermatoptera and Pseudoneuroptera, besides a tenth, nearly complete segment, the rudiments of an eleventh uromere,[138] represented by a tergite forming the supra-anal triangular plate. Well developed jointed cercopoda occur in the Orthoptera and Pseudoneuroptera, while the forceps of Forficula (Dermatoptera) are undoubtedly modified cercopoda. An ovipositor occurs in the Neuroptera (Panorpidæ) and Orthoptera.

The metamorphosis is incomplete in all the orders of Phyloptera except the more recent and higher order, i. e., the Neuroptera (in Erichson's sense), in which the transformations are complete, the pupa being quiescent and wholly unlike the larva.

The relative standing of the four orders of Phyloptera is shown in the table or genealogical tree of the winged insects on page 295.

The sequence of the orders, such as we are compelled to adopt in writing or speaking of them, is difficult to decide upon. Beginning with what on the whole may be regarded as the lowest order, we might first take up the Dermatoptera, which are in most respects the most generalized forms, and stand nearest to the Thysanura (Japyx).

---

[138] NOMENCLATURE OF EXTERNAL PARTS OF ARTHROPODA.—The following terms have been devised for convenience in anatomical and systematic work on the Arthropoda, and are submitted for the judgment of naturalists. We have adopted most of them in a monograph of N. A. Phyllopoda, published in Hayden's Twelfth Annual Report U. S. Geol. Surv. Terr., 1883.

The term arthromere, originally employed in the author's "Guide to the Study of Insects," in 1869, is now restricted to the body-segments of Arthropods, the term zonite or somite being used for the body-segments of worms, etc., as well as Arthropods. The "head," "thorax" and "abdomen" may be termed respectively cephalosome, bænosome (Gr. baino, to walk, locomotion), and urosome. The head-segments are termed cephalomeres, the thoracic segments bænomeres, and the abdominal uromeres. For the antennæ the term æsthopoda, and for the mandibles and maxillæ the previously used term gnathopoda is adopted.

The thoracic legs are termed bænopoda, and Westwood's term uropoda, applied by him to the terminal pairs of feet of the Tetradecapoda, is extended to all the abdominal feet of Arthropods. The basal abdominal feet of male Decapods, modified as accessory reproductive organs, are termed, for convenience in descriptive carcinology, gonopoda, and the jointed anal cerci of certain insects and of Apus are termed cercopoda (κέρκος, tail; πούς, ποδός, foot). The elements of the ovipositor or sting are three pairs of blade-like appendages which are homologues of the legs; they may therefore be designated as oöpoda, as they are chiefly concerned in egg-laying.

The following is the succession of orders, placing the lowest upper-most:

Dermatoptera Burm.
Orthoptera Linn.
Pseudoneuroptera Erichson.
Neuroptera Linn., restricted by Erichson.

Before discussing the relative standing of these orders, we will briefly indicate the more salient and generally applicable differential charac-ters, especially what we regard as the more fundamental ones, but slightly touching upon the mouth-parts and wings, these being peri-pheral and more adaptive characters and liable to greatest variation, and being of less value in characterizing the orders of *Phyloptera*.

ORDER 1. DERMATOPTERA.

Forficula presents so many features separating it from the Ortho-ptera, and is so composite a form, that it should be regarded as the type of a distinct order, in which it was originally placed by Leach, Kirby, Burmeister, and Westwood. Its composite nature is seen both in the elytra and the hind wings, which anticipate the Coleopterous type of wings. On the other hand the larva resembles Japyx, the Thysanuran, with its anal forceps, and in most respects Forficula is the lowest, most decided stem-form of the Phyloptera.

The Dermatoptera are characterized by the flatness of the body, and the large terminal forceps. The head is flat, horizontal in position, while the presence of the V-shaped epicranial suture is a sign of inferi-ority, as it is characteristic of Thysanura and Platypteran larvæ as well as Coleopterous larvæ. The remarkable thoracic structure, which is described farther on, as well as the curious overlapping of the abdom-inal tergites, forbid our uniting the Dermatoptera with the Orthoptera. The small, short elytra, and the very large, rounded, longitudinally and once-cross-folded hind wings, which remind us rather of the Coleoptera than Orthoptera, are also important diagnostic features. Finally, the metamorphosis of the Dermatoptera is even less complete than that of the Orthoptera.

The ligula (Pl. XXIII, Fig. 6) is bifid, being divided into a pair of two-jointed paraglossæ. The labium is thus similar to that of the Ortho-ptera, though scarcely more like them than like Termes.

ORDER 2. ORTHOPTERA.

The head is more or less vertical in position; the front is very large, broad, and long, the epicranial region very large and often hypertrophied. The clypeus is large and subdivided as in Pseudoneuroptera. In the Orthoptera, as a rule, the deeply-cleft ligula is indistinctly four-lobed, the outer pair of paraglossæ very well developed, while the inner pair is minute or undeveloped, as in the Acrydii, especially Caloptenus;

but in the Locustariæ the ligula is four-lobed, and in the Gryllidæ decidedly so. In the Mantidæ and Blattariæ the ligula is plainly four-lobed, nearly as much so as in the Termitidæ. In the Phasmidæ the ligula is intermediate in form between the Mantidæ and Locustariæ.

The prothorax is usually remarkably large, particularly the notum. The meso- and metanotum exactly repeat each other, and the metanotum is usually (Acrydii and Locustariæ) longer and larger than the mesonotum, the hind wings being almost uniformly much larger than the anterior pair. The pleurites are very large and square as well as high, the episterna and epimera being large and oblong and equally developed. The sternites are very large and broad. The coxæ are sometimes (Blatta) very large; the hind legs in the Acrydii are much larger than the anterior pairs. The fore wings are narrower than the hinder pair, and show a slight tendency to become subelytriform; on the other hand the hind wings are very large and broad, distinctly net-veined, with numerous longitudinal veins, and they fold up longitudinally.

The abdomen has eleven uromeres, the eleventh forming a triangular tergite. The cercopoda are often (Blatta, Mantis, &c.) multi-articulate and well developed, while the ovipositor is often large and perfect. The metamorphosis is more incomplete than in the Pseudoneuroptera.

With the exclusion of the Forficulariæ, the Orthoptera, as here restricted, are a tolerably well circumscribed group; and though there are great structural differences between the families, yet the connection or sequence of the families from the Blattariæ through the Phasmidæ and Mantidæ and Acrydii to the Locustariæ, and, finally, the highest family, the Gryllidæ, is one which can be distinctly perceived. There is no occasion for a subdivision of the order into groups higher than families, as the Blattariæ are but a family removed from the Mantidæ.

Order 3. PSEUDONEUROPTERA Erichson.

It is difficult, if not impossible, to satisfactorily characterize by a sharp-cut definition this very elastic order. As regards the thorax, there is no uniformity in the structure that we have been able to discover, nor is there in the structure of the wings, nor more than a general resemblance in the mouth-parts.

The definition of the Pseudoneuroptera in Hagen's Synopsis of the Neuroptera of North America, as given in the analytical table, which is stated in a foot-note to have been prepared at the request of the Smithsonian Institution by Baron Osten Sacken, gives no fundamental characters based on a study of the trunk. Those mentioned are what we have called peripheral characters, i. e., those drawn from the mouth-parts, wings, and appendages. So far as we know, no satisfactory definition of the Pseudoneuroptera has ever been given. In Hagen's Synopsis, among the other superficial characters given, are these: "Lower lip mostly cleft"; "antennæ either subulate and thin, the tarsi three- to five-articulate; or setiform, or filiform, in which case the tarsi are two- to four-articulate."

These characters, though superficial, are the most important yet presented, perhaps (disregarding the metamorphosis), for separating the Pseudoneuroptera from the genuine Neuroptera. But the cleft labium is also to be found in Orthoptera; and among the Orthoptera, which usually have five-jointed tarsi, the Mantidæ have four tarsal joints. The Perlidæ, Odonata, and Ephemerina have been, by Gerstäcker (Peters and Carus' Zoologie), associated with the Orthoptera under the name *Orthoptera amphibiotica*, but such an alliance does not seem to us to be entirely a natural or convenient one; it is simply transferring a mass of heterogeneous forms to what, as now limited, is a natural and well circumscribed category, and yet we confess that it is difficult to give diagnostic adult characters separating the Pseudoneuroptera from the Orthoptera, though the general facies of the Orthoptera is quite unlike that of the the Pseudoneuroptera.

In the Pseudoneuroptera, beginning with the more generalized forms, the Perlidæ and Termitidæ, the labium (second maxillæ) is deeply cleft, the cleft not, however, in these or any other insects, extending to the mentum, or even clear through the palpiger. Each lobe is also cleft, so that the ligula is really four-lobed; the outer lobes are called by Gerstäcker[139] the "lamina externa," and the inner the "lamina interna." These finger-shaped, non-articulated, fleshy lobes appear to be homologous with, or at least suggest the outer pair of, paraglossæ of the Coleoptera and Hymenoptera. In the Perlidæ (Pl. XL, fig. 6) the four lobes of the ligula are well developed, and the lobes of the inner pair are broader than the outer. In the Termitidæ (Pl. XLI, figs. 2, 3) the lobes are well developed, but the inner pair of lobes is either one-half or not quite so wide as the outer paraglossæ; the palpiger is cleft. In the Embidæ, according to Savigny's figures, the ligula is four-lobed, but the inner pair is narrow and rudimentary.

In the Odonata, according to Gerstäcker's excellent drawings, the ligula varies much. In Gomphus it is entire; in some of the higher Libellulinæ only two-lobed; but in Æschna it is four-lobed, the outer lobe slender; but separate from the palpus. In Calopteryx the ligula is widely cleft, the two inner lobes are wide apart, while the outer pair is consolidated with the labial palpi. Owing to the specialized nature of the labial palpi, the mouth-parts of the Odonata are sufficiently *sui generis* and distinctive to prevent their being placed among the Orthoptera, even if the thorax were not so dissimilar. In the aborted labium and other mouth-parts of the Ephemerina we also have strongly-marked characteristics forbidding their being placed in the Orthoptera; were it not for the strong resemblance of the Termitidæ to the Orthoptera (Blattariæ,) probably no one would have thought of carrying the Pseudoneuroptera over into the Orthoptera.

The relative proportion of the head and sclerites varies greatly; no

[139] Zur Morphologie der Orthoptera amphibiotica. Aus der Festschrift zur Gesellsch. Naturforsch. Freunde. 1873.

general rule can be laid down as to the relative proportions of the epicranium and of the clypeus, or of the gular region.

On this account I had at one time decided to split the group into two, and to restrict Erichson's *Pseudoneuroptera* to the Platyptera,[140] and to adopt Latreille's term *Subulicornia* for the Odonata and Ephemerina (*Subulicornes* of Latreille). It may, however, be best, for the sake of clearness, to retain Erichson's order *Pseudoneuroptera* as he indicated it, and to dismember it into what may be regarded, provisionally at least, as three suborders:

1. *Platyptera* (Termitidæ, Embidæ, Psocidæ, and Perlidæ:=Corrodentia and Orthoptera amphibiotica in part).

2. *Odonata* (Libellulidæ).

3. *Ephemerina* (Ephemeridæ).

It is comparatively easy to give well-grounded differential characters for these three suborders. They are so distinct that they may perhaps hereafter be regarded as entitled to the rank of orders, or the *Pseudoneuroptera* may be dismembered into the Pseudoneuroptera and Subulicornia (Odonata and Ephemerina).

1. *Platyptera.*—The body is flattened; the head horizontal. The pronotum is large, broad, and square. The meso- and metanotum are remarkable on account of the imperfect differentiation of the scutum and scutellum; the latter is indefinite in outline, but very large. The flanks (pleurites) are, when long, oblique, or are short. The sternites are usually very large and broad. There are often eleven uromeres.

2. *Odonata.*—While the Odonata and Ephemerina are somewhat alike as regards the form and venation of the fore wings, in their mouth-parts and thorax they are entirely unlike. The Odonata are remarkable for the great dorsal (tergal) development of the mesepisterna and the enormous development of the meso- and metapleurites in general, while the notum of the meso- and metathorax, though of the same type as the Orthoptera, is minute in size. The prothorax is very small, both dorsally and on the sides, forming a collar.

The wings are as markedly net-veined as in the Orthoptera, though the hinder pair are not folded longitudinally as in that order. The Odonata literally live on the wing, and thus the shape of the sclerites of the notum of the wing-bearing segments approaches that of the Orthoptera, although the prothorax is remarkably small compared with that of the Orthoptera, and forbids their union with this order, as was done by Gerstäcker and other German entomologists. The head of the Odonata is remarkable for the enormous size of the eyes and the consequent great reduction in size of the epicranium, as compared with the large epicranium of the Orthoptera. The mouth-parts are like those of the Orthoptera, except that the second maxillæ form a ro-

---

[140] This name πλατύς, flat, πτερόν, wing, in allusion to the wings which in the majority (the Psocidæ folding their wings rather roof-like) fold their wings flat on the back. The Isoptera of Brullé comprise the Termitidæ alone.

markable, mask-like labium. The abdomen is very long, slender and cylindrical; there are eleven uromeres, the eleventh being well represented, while the cercopoda are not jointed, but in the form of claspers.

3. *Ephemerina.*—In the small epicranium, and the large male eyes, the Ephemerina resemble the Odonata, though the rudimentary mouth-parts are in plan entirely unlike them. So, also, the prothorax is small and annular, but the subspherical, concentrated thorax is remarkable for the large mesothorax and the small metathorax. Hence the hind wings are small and sometimes obsolete. The long, slender abdomen has ten uromeres, and bears, besides the two long, filamental multiarticulate cercopoda, a third median one.

The larvæ of the lower Odonata and of the Ephemeridæ closely approach in form those of the Perlidæ, showing that the three suborders here mentioned probably had a common ancestry, which can be theoretically traced to a form not remote from Campodea. By reason of the general resemblance of the larval forms of these three suborders it would be inadvisable to separate the Odonata and Ephemerina from the Platyptera, although, when we consider the adult forms alone, there would appear to be some grounds for such a division.

Order 4. NEUROPTERA.

The head is horizontal and somewhat flattened, except in the Trichoptera and Panorpidæ, where it is subspherical and vertical. The body shows a tendency to be round or cylindrical, the thorax being more or less spherical, but there is great diversity in form from the Sialidæ to the Trichoptera. The mouth-parts are free and the mandibles well developed, except in the Trichoptera, where the mandibles are nearly obsolete in form, and functionless, thus suggesting or anticipating the Lepidoptera.

In the Neuroptera the ligula is entirely unlike any of the foregoing and lower groups. It is entire, forming a broad, flat, large, rounded lobe; it is largest in Myrmeleon, Ascalaphus, and Mantispa, but smaller in Corydalis, where it is also narrower, and indented on the front edge.

In Panorpa the ligula is minute, rudimentary (Pl. LIX, fig. 7). In the Trichoptera it is also minute and rudimentary (Pl. LIX, fig. 5).

The prothorax is usually (Planipennia) large, broad, and square, but is ring- or collar-like in the Trichoptera, being short and small, much as in Lepidoptera. Except in the Trichoptera, the meso- and metanotum are characterized by the large, cordate præscutum, and in the Hemerobina the metascutum is partially or (in Ascalaphus) wholly cleft, the præscutum and scutellum meeting on the median line of the thorax.

In the Hemerobina and Sialidæ the metathorax is as large, or nearly as large, as the mesothorax, and the hind wings are as large as the anterior pair. The wings are not net-veined, the type of venation being entirely unlike that of the Orthoptera and Pseudoneuroptera. The costal space is wide and well marked, and the transverse veinlets are few and far apart, compared with the two orders just mentioned.

The abdomen is cylindrical, and there are 9-10 uromeres. The ovipositor is only developed in Raphidia, while the cercopoda are not developed. The metamorphosis is complete, as in the Lepidoptera, etc., the pupa being entirely unlike the larva, and quiescent, often protected by a cocoon or case. The order may be divided into two suborders:

1. *Planipennia* (Sialidæ, Hemerobiidæ, Panorpidæ).
2. *Trichoptera* (Phryganeidæ).

The following tabular view and diagram will in a degree express our views as to the classification of the orders of the Hexapodous or winged insects, with especial reference to the Pseudoneuroptera, the order perhaps the most difficult to bring in relation with the other Phyloptera. The diagram will also serve to express our conceptions of the genealogy of the Hexapodous orders.

View of the grand divisions of winged insects (Hexapoda).

Superorders.	Orders.	Suborders.
Euglossata [141]	{ Hymenoptera .... { Lepidoptera .... { Diptera	{ Diptera (genuina). { Aphaniptera. { Pupipara.
Elytrophora [142]	Coleoptera..............	{ Coleoptera (genuina). { Strepsiptera.
Eurhynchota [143]	Hemiptera	{ Homoptera. { Heteroptera. { Physapoda. { Mallophaga.
	{ Neuroptera	{ Trichoptera. { Planipennia.
Phyloptera	{ Pseudoneuroptera	{ Odonata. { Ephemerina. { Platyptera.
	Orthoptera............. Dermatoptera..........	
Synaptera [144]	Thysanura	{ Cinura. { Symphyla. { Collembola.

[141] We propose the name *Euglossata* for the highest insects, comprising those orders which, besides having the mouth parts (either the first or second maxillæ, or both) modified so as to sip, suck or lap up liquid food, also have the body cylindrical, and the thorax more or less spherical and concentrated

[142] This term is proposed for the Coleoptera, which are nearly equivalent to the other superorders, being a remarkably circumscribed group.

[143] This term is proposed for the Hemiptera, in all of which, except the Mallophaga and Physapoda (Thrips), the mouth parts are united to form a sucking beak.

[144] This term is proposed for the Thysanuran apterous Hexapoda which are perhaps nearly the morphological equivalents of either of the four other superorders.

GENEALOGY OF THE INSECTS (HEXAPODA).

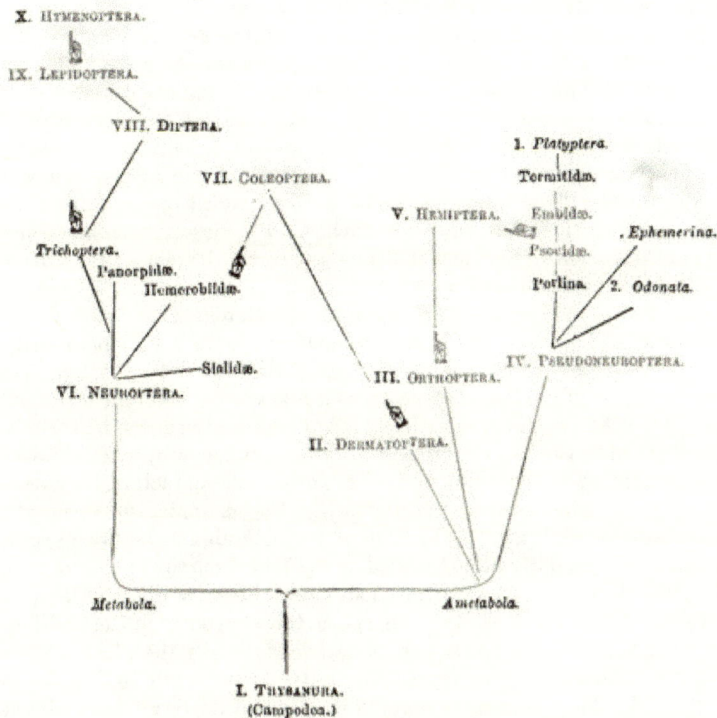

X. HYMENOPTERA.

IX. LEPIDOPTERA.

VIII. DIPTERA.

1. *Platyptera.*

Termitidæ.

VII. COLEOPTERA.

V. HEMIPTERA. Emblidæ. *. Ephemerina.*

Psocidæ.

Trichoptera.

Panorphidæ. Perlina. 2. *Odonata.*

Hemerobiidæ.

Sialidæ. IV. PSEUDONEUROPTERA.

VI. NEUROPTERA. III. ORTHOPTERA.

II. DERMATOPTERA.

Metabola. Ametabola.

I. THYSANURA.
(Campodea.)

GENEALOGY OF THE HEXAPODA.

I. *Thysanura.*—This order once comprised some lost types nearly resembling Lepisma, Campodea, and Japyx, and more especially Scolopendrella, the probable stem-form of the Hexapoda. In other words, from a
hypothetical form resembling Campodea or Scolopendrella, it is not difficult to suppose that all or at least the majority of Hexapoda took their
origin. It is possible that by a few intermediate steps now lost, Forficula may have descended from the Thysanuran Japyx; this is suggested
by the form of the body, the head with its V-shaped suture, and the abdomen with its forceps, so like that of Japyx. The genus Lepisma is a
rather more specialized form than Campodea, and Machilis is still more
so, as proved by its mouth parts and the presence of compound eyes.
Scolopendrella, with its abdominal true legs, comes nearer to our hypothetical form than even Campodea. The group of *Poduridæ* (Collem-
bola) is most probably a series of degradational forms, originally sprung
from a higher, more generalized, Campodea-like ancestor.

II. *Dermatoptera.*—This order, represented by but one family, differs,
as already stated, from the Orthoptera, with which it is usually classi-

fied, much more than the Termitidæ. It stands alone, and, as observed, its larvæ closely resemble the Thysanuran Japyx.

III. *Orthoptera.*—After the elimination of the Forficulidæ from the Orthoptera, we have a natural and easily circumscribed group. Beginning with decidedly the most generalized and at the same time lowest family, the Blattariæ, followed by the Mantidæ, which have a number of characters which recall the Blattariæ, we pass up through the Phasmidæ to the typical family, the Acrydii; then succeed the Locustariæ, and finally the Gryllidæ, which on the whole are farthest removed from the stem-forms of the order, the Cockroaches. The close resemblance of a larval Cockroach to Lepisma indicates the direct descent of the Orthoptera from the Cinurous Thysanura.

IV. *Pseudoneuroptera.*—This is the most heterogeneous order or assemblage of insects. While it is comparatively easy to circumscribe the Neuroptera (taken in Erichson's sense), and the Orthoptera as here restricted, the group Pseudoneuroptera is remarkably heterogeneous and elastic. We have failed to satisfactorily diagnose the order as a whole. The Termitidæ connect the Orthoptera and Pseudoneuroptera so closely that, excepting in the wings and other peripheral characters, they seem but a family removed from the Blattariæ. For example, the Termitidæ resemble the Blattariæ in the form of the epicranium, in the clypeus, which is but partially differentiated at the base from the epicranium, in the form of the labrum, and the small eyes as well as the mouth-parts.

In the thorax the Termitidæ approach the Blattariæ in the undifferentiated senta of the meso- and metathorax; while the pleurites are also very oblique and the femora are flattened and ovate in form, as in Blatta. In the abdomen, as regards the form of the tergites, as well as the urites and pleurites, besides the form of the end of the abdomen and of the cercopoda, the Termitidæ closely approach the Blattariæ. The degree of metamorphosis is also the same.

On the other hand, the close relationship of the Termitidæ to the Embidæ, as well as to the Psocidæ and also the Perlidæ, and the close resemblance of the Perlid larvæ to those of Odonata and Ephemerina, forbid our removing the Platyptera from the Pseudoneuroptera.

We conclude, then, that the Ephemerina, Odonata, Platyptera, as well as Orthoptera and Dermatoptera have had a common origin from some Thysanuran stock. It is possible that these five groups are nearly equivalent and should take the rank of orders, but the classification we have given in the tabular view on p. 294 may better express their relations.

The Odonata and Ephemerina are, as regards the wings and metamorphosis, a good deal alike. The Ephemerina, while having a highly concentrated thorax, are, as regards the mouth-parts and hind wings, degradational forms, the result of probable degeneration from a primitive, lost form. From what group the Ephemerina may have originated it seems to us impossible to conjecture.

V. *Hemiptera.*—The only clew to the origin of this well circumscribed order is the fact that in the Physapoda (Thrips) and the Mallophaga the mandibles are free and adapted for biting. This would indicate that the entire group was derived from ancestors allied possibly to the Phyloptera. The Mallophaga are by different authors referred to the Orthoptera and Neuroptera, but the development of the bird-lice as worked out by Melnikow fully proves that in the form of the egg, the mode of development, and general form of the embryo, the Parasita and Mallophaga travel along the same developmental path until just before hatching, when in Mallophaga the jaws remain free, while in the Parasita they become farther modified and form a sucking beak.

There is a possibility that the Hemiptera may have descended from insects remotely allied to the Pseudoneuroptera; perhaps forms resembling the Psocidæ; at least this family, the wingless forms of which superficially resemble the Mallophaga, gives hints which may throw light on the origin of the Hemiptera. They are evidently the offshoot of a stock which had an incomplete metamorphosis, or they may have descended directly from a modified Campodea-like ancestral form.

VI. *Neuroptera.*—The members of this order are, excepting perhaps the Hemiptera, the most modern and least composite or synthetic forms that we have yet met with in our ascent up the insect series from the Thysanura. Moreover, in them for the first time do we meet with worm-like, cylindrical-bodied larvæ, or what we have called eruciform larvæ.[145] These larvæ are secondary forms, derived, as Fritz Müller has in a general way suggested, from those larvæ which have an incomplete metamorphosis. By what line of descent, however, the lowest group of Neuroptera, viz., the Sialidæ, arose, it would be difficult to say. The earliest winged insects were probably terrestrial; the aquatic larval forms of the Sialidæ are evidently derivations from Campodea-like terrestrial larvæ. But how the perfect metamorphosis with the quiescent pupa of the Neuroptera was brought about, is indeed a problem. It is evident, however, that the eruciform larva is a derivation from a Thysanuriform[146] type, first stated by Fritz Müller.

It seems to us that a consideration of the diverse larval forms which occur in the present order, throws some light on the origin of a complete metamorphosis in insects in general. In the Sialidæ, as the larva of Corydalus, or Semblis, we have a Campodea-form provided with gills, and with the mouth-parts adapted for seizing and biting its prey. The terrestrial larvæ of the Hemerobiidæ are evidently modifications of the Sialid larval form; the differences of structure in them, such as the long,

---

[145] See "Our Common Insects," p. 175, 1873. Also the American Naturalist, vol. V, Sept. 1871.

[146] We have in the writings just quoted called the second class of larvæ Leptiform, but the term Thysanuriform, or Brauer's expression Campodea form, is preferable. The Campodea or primitive Hexapodous form is evidently a derivative form, which points back to a common six-footed ancestor of all Tracheata, to which the term *Leptiform* may be applied.

slender mandibles and maxillæ and the short abdomen, being the result
of their carnivorous habits, and their being obliged to climb up the stems
of plants or to walk over the leaves after smaller insects.   Under such
circumstances the body would become shorter and more concentrated, and
the legs well developed.   In the Trichoptera, whose larvæ live in cylindrical cases, the body is seen to be essentially Campodea-like; the head
is fundamentally like that of Corydalis; the differences are adaptive.

But when we regard the larva of the Panorpidæ, we are dealing with
a new type; it is caterpillar-like, cruciform; its body is slender and cylindrical, the head small, and feet short and small.   Notice also its
habits.   The larva of *Panorpa communis* of Europe, as described by
Brauer,[147] is remarkably caterpillar-like or cruciform.   The head is small,
well rounded, and the antennæ and mouth-parts are small and rudimentary, compared with those of other Neuroptera, not excepting the Trichoptera.   Moreover, they are constructed on nearly the same type as
those of caterpillars; for example, the mandibles are short, toothed, of
the same form as in Lepidopterous larvæ; the maxillæ are short, and
whether more than two-lobed Brauer does not state, though his figure
indicates apparently a rudimentary third lobe; the palpi are four-jointed,
while the labium is small with small three-jointed palpi.

The form of the body is thick and stout, like that of a Bombycid
(Arctian) larva.   The short, four-jointed thoracic feet are in length and
thickness like those of caterpillars.   But the most striking resemblance
to caterpillars and saw-fly larvæ is seen in the eight pairs of abdominal feet, which Brauer describes as conical or pin-shaped (kegelför-
mig), while on the last (ninth or tenth ?) segment are four finger-shaped,
equal processes.   Not only the form of the body, but also the arrangement and shape of the button-like setiferous warts on the body are
strikingly like those of some Arctian caterpillars.   The pupa has free
limbs and wings as in other Neuroptera.   The larva of Panorpa bores
an inch deep into moss-covered, not wet soil.

The larvæ of Bittacus (*B. italicus* and *hagenii*), as also described and
figured by Brauer,[148] have a rounded head, with small mouth-parts; the
mandibles are, however, rather long, compared with those of Panorpa;
while the maxillæ have apparently two inner short lobes, and a four-
jointed, short maxillary palpus; the labium is rudimentary, with a pair
of short, minute, two-jointed palpi.   The body is not so thick as in Panorpa; it is cylindrical and adorned with long, scattered, dorsal spines,
which bear one or two branches near the base, while there is a lateral
row of slender filaments, and a row of ventral verticillate hairs.   It thus
bears a resemblance to the larvæ of some butterflies, as *Vanessa antiopa*,
and especially the young Polyommatus (*Ilcodes hypophleas*) or the Bombycid larvæ of *Anisota stigma* or Platysamia, as well as Selandria

---

[147] Sitzungsberichte math.-naturw. Classe k. Akad. Wiss. Wien. 1851.   Tafel 1.
[148] Verhandlungen k. k. zool.-bot. Gesellschaft in Wien. 1871.

larvæ. Brauer's figures show a pair of abdominal, two-jointed feet to each of the nine abdominal segments, while just as in Lepidopterous larvæ and in that of Panorpa there is a pair of prothoracic spiracles, none on the mesothoracic or metathoracic segments, and there are nine pairs of abdominal spiracles according to Brauer's figure, or one more pair than in Lepidopterous larvæ.

The fact that there are in the larval Panorpidæ collectively a pair of feet to each abdominal segment (the terminal segment in Panorpa bearing what are evidently homologues of the anal proplegs of caterpillars) is of much significance when we bear in mind that while no caterpillars are known to have more than five pairs of abdominal or proplegs, some of the segments bearing none, yet the embryos, as shown by Kowalevsky, have temporary embryonic indications of legs, a pair to each segment (uromere); it is a significant fact that the cruciform larvæ of the Panorpidæ actually have two-jointed legs to each abdominal segment, the penultimate segment in Bittacus bearing such legs, and the terminal segment bearing leg-like processes in Panorpa. The origin of the Lepidoptera from the same stem-form as the Panorpidæ thus seems a reasonable hypothesis.

In the metamorphosis of Mantispa, as Brauer has shown, there is a hypermetamorphosis, i. e., two larval stages. The first stage is Campodeaform; but the second is sub-cruciform. The transformations of Mantispa appear to give us the key to the mode in which a metamorphosis was brought about. The larva, born a Campodea-like form, active, with large, long, four-jointed feet, living a sedentary life in the egg-sac of a spider, before the first molt loses the use of its feet, while the antennæ are partly aborted. The fully grown larva is round-bodied, with small, caterpillar-like feet and a small, round head. Its external appendages retrograding and retarded, acceleration of growth goes on within, and thus the pupal form is perfected while the larva is full-fed and quiescent; hence as a result the pupal stage became a quiescent one, and by inheritance it gradually became a permanent habit characteristic of Neuroptera, all of which have a complete metamorphosis, and hence inherited by all the orders of metabolic insects which probably originated from Neuroptera-like forms, and the imago represents a highly accelerated stage.

When we consider the imagos or adult Neuroptera: the small, collar-like prothorax, the spherical, concentrated thorax as a whole, and the cylindrical abdomen, are features which give them a comparatively specialized and modern aspect. Without doubt the Neuropterous labium (Plate LIII) is a secondary product compared with that of the Orthoptera or the Platyptera, where it is deeply cleft (Plate XXVII.) It will be remembered that in the embryo of all insects the labium or second maxillæ originates like the first pair.

Origin of the Coleoptera.—Although the beetles are a remarkably homogeneous and well circumscribed order, there are certain larval forms and life-histories which point out with a tolerable degree of certainty the line of development of this extensive order from the Campodea type. There are two series of facts which seem to us to throw light on the subject.

First, the form of the free, active larvæ of the carnivorous groups of beetles. The larvæ of the Carabidæ, Dytiscidæ and Staphylinidæ appear to us to be on the whole more nearly allied to what was probably the primitive form of Coleopterous larva than those of any other families. This ancestral Coleopterous larva was probably directly related to the Campodea-form ancestor of the Hexapoda. The general form of the body, the homonomous segments, the free, biting, toothed mandibles, the well-developed one- or two-lobed maxillæ with their three-jointed palpi, and the well-developed second maxillæ (labium), also the four-jointed antennæ, and the presence of ocelli, while showing that the existing carnivorous larvæ are the most specialized and highly developed, also show that they have undergone the least modification from the primitive type of Coleopterous larva. In the scavenger larval forms, as the Silphidæ, Dermestidæ and allied families, the mouth-parts begin to be modified and less developed, and the form of the body undergoes a change, becoming thicker and with less developed feet.

In the Elateridæ and Searabæidæ, which in general are phytophagous, we see a still more decided change; the body becoming cylindrical and the mouth-parts more aberrant.

In the wood-boring Buprestidæ and Cerambycidæ, and in the leaf-eating Chrysomelid larvæ, we witness a decided departure from the carnivorous type; the mouth-parts show a tendency to become more or less aborted, the legs are frequently wanting and the body more or less maggot-like. Finally, the tendency to a gradual degradation and atrophy of the head, mouth-parts and legs culminates in the grubs of the weevils (Curculionidæ and Scolytidæ), placing them at the foot of the Coleopterous series, and shows that they have undergone the greatest modification of form, and have become adapted to conditions the most unlike those which constituted the environment of the primitive Coleopterous larva.

The relative form of the maxillæ appears to be a good index as to the general development of the body in the different groups of Coleoptera, especially those standing above the wood-boring families. The facts may, for convenience, be arranged in the following form:

Cicindelidæ.—Maxilla with a maxillary lobe or *mala* proper ending in a 2-jointed appendage which is longer than the 3-jointed palpus. (Antennæ 4-jointed; 3 ocelli.)

Carabidæ.—Maxilla with the mala 2-jointed; maxillary palpus 4-jointed. (Antennæ 4-jointed, bifurcate; ocelli often present.)

Dytiscidæ (and Hydradephaga in general).—Maxilla with the mala absent; the palpi 4-jointed.

The maxilla in the aquatic forms of the Carabid type is only a modification of the Geodephagous maxilla; the terminal palpal joint being acute and raptorial.

Staphylinidæ.—Maxilla with a 1-jointed inner lobe (Xantholinus), or the mala broad and setose as in the succeeding families (Platystethus and especially Bledius); maxillary palpi 3- and 4 jointed.

The Staphylinid type of maxilla is simply a modification of the Carabid, with a tendency to degeneration in the lower genera (Bledius, etc). Many larvæ in this family are carnivorous.

Elateridæ.—Maxilla with a 2-jointed lobe or mala; the maxillary palpus 4 jointed. Antennæ 4-jointed, bifurcate as in Carabid larvæ; mandibles toothed. The maxillæ of Elater and Athous are free. While generally supposed to be vegetable-eaters (as Agriotes), those larvæ which live under the bark of trees in mines made by Longicorn and other borers have been shown by Ratzeburg, Dufour and Perris to be in part carnivorous, living on Dipterous and Longicorn larvæ, as well as on the excrementitious vegetable matter filling the burrows. Perris (*Insectes du Pin maritime*, p. 190) has pointed out the close resemblance of the mouth-parts of this family to those of the larval Carabidæ.

In the Scarabæidæ, Buprestidæ, and all the lower families of Coleoptera, the maxillæ are of a rather simpler type than in the foregoing families; the maxillary lobe, or mala, being simple and more or less fringed with stiff hairs. In the Scarabæidæ (Osmoderma), and in Pyrochroa, which is carnivorous, the mouth-parts are as complicated as in any; but in the Buprestidæ and Chrysomelidæ they are less developed, while they are most rudimentary in form and size in the wood-boring weevils and Scolytids; the antennæ and second maxillæ and legs also share in the degradation of structure consequent on the burrowing lignivorous habits of the larvæ.

But it is in the so-called hypermetamorphosis of the Meloidæ, that of the blister beetle (Epicauta) as well as Hornia having been fully described and illustrated by Professor Riley in the First Report of the United States Entomological Commission (p. 297–302, Pl. IV), that we have a clew to the probable origin of the different types of Coleopterous larvæ. The metamorphosis of the oil beetle (Meloë) originally discovered by Siebold and Newport and also Fabre, is described in different entomological manuals.[19] In brief, the larvæ of Meloë when hatched are very minute, active, six-legged, slender-bodied creatures, parasitic on wild bees; as the legs end in three claws the insects in this stage are called "triungulins." These larvæ attached to the bees are thus carried into the nests of the latter, where they feed on the bee-larvæ and bee-bread. On becoming fully fed, instead of transforming directly into the pupa state, they assume a second (coarctate) larval form, entirely unlike the first, the body being cylindrical and motionless, with long legs; they then attain a third larval stage, the head small and the body thick, cylindrical and footless; after this they assume a true pupa stage, and finally become beetles.

Professor Riley has traced the hypermetamorphosis of the blister

---

[19] See the writer's "Guide to the Study of Insects," pp. 477–479, figs. 447–451.

beetle (Epicauta), which passes through three larval stages before transforming to a pupa. He divides the life-history of this beetle into the following stages: (1) Triungulin; (2) second larva (*a*, Carabidoid; *b*, ultimate or Scarabæidoid stage); (3) pseudo-pupa, or coarctate larva; (4) third larva (closely resembling the Scarabæidoid stage of second); (5) true pupa; (6) beetle. (The reader should examine the figures in Pl. IV of the First Report; otherwise he cannot understand the following remarks.)

It appears, then, that the first larva, or triungulin, in form resembles the Campodea-like primitive larval form of Coleoptera; the Epicauta triungulin closely resembles a Carabid larva, the head, antennæ, and mouth-parts, as well as the legs and form of the body in general, being on the primitive, Carabid type (somewhat like Casnonia (?), Galerita and Harpalus); the second larva, *a*, Carabidoid stage, though quite different as regards the mouth-parts, and with a smaller head, thicker body and much shorter legs, still adheres to the higher Carabid form (Carabus and allies). During the Scarabæidoid stage the second larva rests nearly motionless in the egg of the locust, and is like the curved, clumsy larvæ of the cockchafer or June beetle and other Lamellicorn larvæ, which also have the similar habits of lying still in their burrows and feeding on the roots of grass, or, as in the case of Osmoderma, lying nearly motionless in their cells in rotten wood. This sort of life going on, the larval blister beetle after six or seven days assumes the ultimate stage of the second larva, and now, from apparent continued disuse, the mouth-parts and legs become more aborted than before, and the insect in this stage may be compared to some Longicorn larvæ, with a general resemblance in the curved, cylindrical body to the Ptinid and Chrysomelid, and it even approximates in general shape Curculionid larvæ. In the pseudo-pupa or coarctate larva this process of disuse and obsolescence of parts culminates in the immobile stage preceding (with the intervention of third larva) the pupal condition. We thus see that in the life-history of a single species of beetle, change in habits or environment, as well as in the food, induces change in the form of the body; and this series of changes in the Meloidæ typifies the successive steps in the degradation of form which characterize the series of Coleopterous larvæ from the Carabidæ down to the Curculionidæ and Scolytidæ. At first all larvæ were carnivorous and active in their habits, with large mandibles and well developed accessory jaws and legs; certain forms then becoming scavengers, their appendages became, from disuse, less developed; then others, becoming phytophagous, became in some cases still less developed, the jaws shorter and toothless, with corresponding modifications in the other mouth-parts, the antennæ and the legs, while the body became thick, fat and cylindrical; until in the wood-boring and seed- or nut-inhabiting weevils the antennæ and maxillæ became rudimentary, almost disappearing, while the legs utterly vanished. Change of habits and surroundings, with corresponding changes in the form of the body and its appendages, both explain the metamorphosis of insects in general and also the differences between the larval forms of the different orders.

The following view will convey an idea of the larvæ of the Coleopterous families which in a general way correspond to the different larval stages of the Meloidæ; it being understood that the resemblances are suggestive and general, and not to be accepted in a too literal sense.

1. Primitive triungulin stage.	In Meloë more like Campodea than in Epicauta.
	Meloidæ.
	Stylopidæ.
	Cicindelidæ.
2. Carabidoid stage.	Carabidæ, Dytiscidæ, Hydrophilidæ.
	Silphidæ, Nitidulariæ, Dermestidæ, Coccinellidæ, etc.
	Elateridæ, Lampyridæ, Telephoridæ, Cleridæ, Pyrochroidæ.
3. Scarabæidoid stage.	Histeridæ.
	Scarabæidæ.
	Ptinidæ.
4. Coarctate stage, more or less cylindrical and apodous.	Cerambycidæ.
	Tenebrionidæ.
	Mordellidæ.
	Curculionidæ.
	Scolytidæ.

From the facts and considerations which have been presented, we are disposed to believe, subject, of course, to future correction, that the primitive Coleoptera were carnivorous forms, and that the scavenger and phytophagous forms have been derived from them, and are therefore secondary products, and as a whole of more recent origin.

The primitive form of beetle was probably a Staphylinus-like form, with a long, narrow body and rudimentary elytra, and carnivorous in habits. This has been suggested by Brauer,[130] though it occurred to us before meeting with his views.

Though the earliest beetle known is a Carboniferous weevil-like form, yet we imagine the Coleopterous type became established in Devonian or Silurian times, when there may have existed the prototypes of the earwigs and beetles; for the two types may have branched off from some Thysanuran form. On the other hand, the primitive Coleopterous larva may have sprung from some metabolous Neuropterous form. The larva of Gyrinus has a striking resemblance to that of Corydalus and other Sialidæ, so much so that a terrestrial Carabidous form most probably was of Neuropterous origin, as indicated in our diagram.

Origin of the Diptera, Lepidoptera, and Hymenoptera.—The Euglossata probably had a common origin in the first place from the metabolic

---

[130] So wird uns der Staphylinus als eine der ältesten Käferformen gelten, etc. Betrachtungen über die Verwandlung der Insekten im Sinne der Descendenz-Theorie, von F. Brauer, Verh. k. k. zool.-bot. Ges., Wien, 1869, p. 313.

Neuroptera. The Lepidoptera probably originated from the same group from which the Panorpidæ and Trichoptera branched off, and we agree with the opinion of H. Müller,[150] who maintains that the Lepidoptera and Trichoptera "proceed from a common stock," though we should suppose that the Panorpidæ in their larval stage represented forms like the ancestral caterpillar.

The adult structure and larval forms of the Diptera show that they originated from nearly the same stock as the moths. The most perfectly developed Dipterous larvæ are those of the Culicidæ and Tipulidæ; these were probably the primitive forms; the other Dipterous larvæ, notably the larval Muscidæ or maggots, are degradational forms, and the lower Diptera appear to have been degraded or degenerate forms.

The case is different with the Hymenoptera. The saw-fly larvæ represent apparently the primitive larval form; and from their resemblance to caterpillars and Panorpid larvæ, show that the Hymenoptera and Lepidoptera may have had a common origin. The footless larvæ of the parasitic Hymenoptera are correlated with their parasitic mode of life, and the similar forms of the larval wasps and bees show that from disuse their mouth-parts and legs became aborted, and the immobile larvæ became short and thick-bodied. Hence such larvæ should be regarded as secondary, adaptive larval types. The high degree of specialization of the bees' mouth-parts, their concentrated bodies and 4-segmented thorax, with other characters, show that they are the highest, most specialized and modern of all insects.

NOTE.—It should be borne in mind that the embryo bee has a pair of temporary abdominal appendages on each segment (uromere); so also has the Lepidopterous, Coleopterous, and Orthopterous embryo, which points back to a common, Scolopendrella-like type; this also possibly indicating a still earlier, worm-like, Peripatus-like ancestor for Myriopoda and Hexapoda at least, if not Arachnida. For previous discussions as to the origin of insects the reader is referred to the writings of Fritz Müller, Brauer, Lubbock, and the author.

Order II. DERMATOPTERA.

FORFICULIDÆ. Plates XXIII, XXIV.

THE HEAD.

Forficula tæniata Dohrn. (Pl. XXIII, figs. 1–3). The head is horizontal in position, broad and flat, squarish, the sides being parallel. There is a V-shaped epicranial suture, which is more distinct in the larvæ of this genus and in Labia. The epicranium is otherwise simple; no ocelli. The clypeus is simple, being no wider and not much larger than the labrum. The genal ridge prominent; a broad gular region. Behind the

[150] American Naturalist, v, July, 1871, 266. See also the same magazine, Nov., 1871, p. 707–713.

short, broad submentum (and in front of the prosternum) is a free sclerite, with a transverse, median impressed line. (This sclerite may be called the *postgula*, and it may correspond to the præsternal sclerite in Blatta, except that no pleural sclerite is attached to it as in Blatta.) The mentum is very large and flat, as long as broad.

THE THORAX.

Notum.

Pronotum. (Fig. 7.) Large, flat, square, a little longer than broad, and rounded behind.

Mesonotum. (Fig. 8.) Somewhat as in Termes, being almost entirely concealed by the pronotum, which rides over it. It is very short—indeed, remarkably so—no other insects approaching this group in this respect, while the metanotum is remarkably developed. Neither the meso- nor metanotum are so wide as the thorax, a broad margin of membrane bordering the sides.

The mesoscutum forms a very short, transversely sublinear sclerite, with the front edge full and curved, but linear (in a transverse sense) on the sides; behind, it receives the minute, diamond-shaped scutellum, which forms a posterior, spine like projection, which rubs or plays upon the medially chitinous front edge of the metanotum. On each side of the scutellum is a transverse, long, lanceolate-oval, chitinous sclerite, which we are disposed to regard as the divided postscutellum. There is no præscutum, and in front of and behind the mesonotum the thorax is soft and membranous.

Metanotum. (Fig. 8.) There is no præscutum. The scutum is very large, nearly as broad as long, broad in front, narrowing behind, sinuous on the front edge, slightly rounded behind, the surface generally flattened, a little convex, with two parallel, slightly converging median ridges; behind these two ridges is the narrow, longitudinally somewhat oblong scutellum. It is not defined by suture, and I could not decide what it was until I had examined Labia, in which it is more distinctly separated from the scutum; it is thick, dark, with a spine-like projection in front.

The large, long and broad, more or less flat area between the scutum and first uromere we are disposed to regard as, without much doubt, an enormously developed postscutellum, especially as it is much shorter and more like the postscutellum of Labia. Its surface is broken up into areas; from behind the metascutellum two widely diverging ridges pass backward and outward to support the base of the wings.

Pleurum.

The pleurites are remarkable for being extended horizontally, and for the unusual form and relations of the epimera, in these respects suggesting the Coleoptera, and perhaps the Staphylinidæ. The legs

20 E C

are inserted at the posterior end on the side of each segment (bæno-mere), as the coxæ are widely separated by the very large and broad sternites.

Propleurites. (Pl. XXIV, fig. 1.) These are well developed. The episternum is horizontal, flat, subtriangular, narrow, reduced to a point before reaching the coxa. A wedge-shaped, triangular sclerite is wedged in between it and the sternite (this may be regarded as the sub-episternum, though possibly the trochantine, as the coxa is apparently entire, and there is otherwise no trochantine to be found).

The epimerum forms the upper part of the pleurum, and is scale-like, oblong-oval; in front it is narrow, and ends at the anterior margin of the notum. The posterior or upper end of the epimerum is free, rounded, scale-like, as it covers the prothoracic stigma.

The coxa is cylindrical, shorter than broad. I can perceive no suture in it, and think the trochantine is obsolete.

Mesopleurites. (Fig. 2.) These sclerites repeat the form of the pro-pleurites. The segment (bænomere) is not so long, and the sclerites are a little more horizontal. The epimerum is more regularly oblong-oval, with a deep crease or fold below the middle, which extends ob-liquely from near the coxa to the front edge of the epimerum.

The episternum is in this segment, as in the preceding one, divided into two pieces; the sur-episternum is very small and situated in the same plane as and on the side of the anterior end of the sternum. The triangular sub-episternum is more oblique than in the propleurum. The coxa is smaller than in the prothorax.

Metapleurites. (Fig. 3.) The structure of this region is very remark-able, as compared with that of other *Phyloptera*. The episternum is simple, not subdivided as in the pro- and mesopleurum, but represented by an acutely triangular sclerite, the base of which lies next to the coxa, the acute apex reaching only two-thirds the way to the front of the sternum. This reduction in the size of the episternal elements is due to the increase in size of the sternum below and the epimerum above.

The epimerum is enormously developed, extending from the insertion of the hind wings (which is very near that of the anterior pair) back nearly to the middle of the second abdominal segment; it thus forms the side of about half the entire thorax; in situation it is horizontal, its sides vertical, but in front next to the mesocoxæ and sternum it rounds down and under, becoming ventral. (This is a most novel mod-ification of the met-episternum, and as unique as the modification of the mes-episternum in the Odonata.)

Coxæ longer than in the mesothorax, and soldered to the sternum.

Sternum.

The sternal elements are in Forficulidæ remarkably large and broad, the species being essentially runners.

The *prosternum* is subdivided into a single, large intercoxal plate, which is oblong, widening in front, and with the surface slightly convex, and a præsternal area which is again subdivided into a median rounded area (Figs. 10–12, *p st*) flanked posteriorly by two small triangular sclerites (*p' st*).

The *mesosternum* is scutellate in shape, nearly as long as broad, wide in front, narrow and well rounded behind the coxæ.

The *metasternum* is entire, very large, broad and rather full on the surface; it is as broad as long, encroaching on the pleurites, and behind is faintly separated by suture from the first urite.

THE ABDOMEN.

There are ten uromeres with ten urosternites (Pl. XXIV, figs. 7–9); the 8th very large, being four times as long as the 7th; the 9th and 10th each forming a pair of lateral scales, at base of each blade of the forceps, being separated by the median sclerites forming the genital armature. The genitals, forming a median, interforcipate, spine-like sclerite, and present above and below, may represent the 11th uromere. The forceps we are inclined to regard as homologues of the cercopoda in other *Phyloptera*.

In regarding as the first uromere the tergite immediately succeeding what we have described as the meta-postscutellum, we differ from what seems to be Professor Westwood's opinion as to the nature of the thorax. He apparently regards this segment or tergite and pleurite (as the sternal portion is not developed) as a part of the metathorax. This segment is a large, broad sclerite closely connected with the metathorax, being slightly excavated next to the metathorax, and rounded behind. On each side it is separated by suture from a narrow pleurite bearing the large, somewhat kidney-shaped first abdominal stigma. The first pair of abdominal stigmata is large and simple, the chitinous edge forming a plain ridge without any projecting teeth. The second pair of abdominal stigmata is visible; the others are not easily detected, as they are minute, but judging by Westwood's figures there are the usual number, *i. e.*, eight pairs. Westwood states that there are three pairs of thoracic spiracles and seven pairs of abdominal ones. Should it be proved that Forficula has a pair of stigmata to each thoracic segment, it will be a remarkable fact, as there is no insect known (Campodea not excepted) which has a pair on each thoracic segment. But we are inclined to think that Westwood has considered our first abdominal uromere with its large spiracles as a part of the metathorax, and thus he considers the number of pairs of thoracic stigmata as three, and of abdominal ones as seven. We have found a large prothoracic spiracle over the coxa on the posterior end under the posterior corner of the pronotum, and concealed on the side by the lateral, scale-like epimerum. We have detected a pair of mesothoracic spiracles, but none on the metathorax.

The result of our examination of Forficulidæ is that they constitute an ordinal group of Phyloptera, equivalent to the Orthoptera. The larval Forficula is very close to Japyx in the form of the head, the thoracic homonomous segments, in having ten uromeres, in the nature of the forceps, and in the eleventh rudimentary segment. So close is the resemblance that we are somewhat inclined to regard Japyx as a degraded Forficula. When we consider the nature of the head, the elytra-like fore wings, the singular hind wings, which are not net-veined, and the forceps, we see how much unlike the Orthoptera Forficula is. It does not approach Blatta nor Termes. In the character of the wings and the thorax, especially the pleurites, Forficula is suggestive of the Coleoptera, though differing from them in being ametabolous.

In Labia the head is as in Forficula. The body being much shorter and thicker than in Forficula, there are some relative differences from what has been described in Forficula.

Notum.

The *pronotum* is shorter and broader, but still covers the *mesonotum;* the latter is as in Forficula, the scutellum being similarly spine-like. The *metanotum* is as in Forficula, with no important differences; the scutellum is rather more distinct, however, but the postscutellum is much shorter, and has similar, lateral, submembranous folds in front.

The first uromere, with its spiracle, is much as in Forficula, while the succeeding uromeres are much shorter.

Pleurum.

The prothoracic pleurites (episternum and epimerum) are as in Forficula, but shorter and broader.

In the mesothorax the epimerum is much rounded, being, with the episternum, rather shorter than in Forficula.

The mesothoracic pleurites are as in Forficula, but much shorter and wider in proportion.

Sternum.

The sternites are not essentially different from those of Forficula, but are rather shorter and broader.

THE LARVA OF FORFICULA (Pl. XXIV).

The notum of each segment is, as in all Orthopterous larvæ, simple, not being differentiated into scutum, scutellum, etc. On the other hand, the sternites and pleurites are as in the adult, and this proves that the tergites are concerned in and modified by the development of the wings. The episterna are subdivided as in the adult.

In the abdomen there are eleven uromeres, but the first tergite is wanting, the urosternite being present, while the eleventh tergite is small and rudimentary.

Order III. ORTHOPTERA. Plates XXV–XXXVIII.

BLATTARIÆ.

THE HEAD.

Blatta americana ♀. The head is held vertically. The epicranium is broad and smooth; the ocelli are absent or obsolete. The clypeus is broad and short, no suture separating it from the epicranium. The genæ are large, a genal ridge separating the genæ from the orbits. The gula is broad and short.

THE THORAX. (Plate XXVI.)

Notum.

The *pronotum* (Pl. XXVIII) is broad and flat, as long as broad.

The *mesonotum* (Pl. XXX) is remarkably broad and flat, two-thirds as long as broad. The præscutum is wanting (unless represented by a transverse strip in front?). The scutum is flat, consisting of two square sclerites separated slightly by the rudimentary scutellum, which latter is lanceolate, narrow, triangular, and divided into two portions, *i. e.*, the posterior or scutellum proper, which is subquadrate, broader than long, and a narrow, long continuation which reaches to the front edge of the scutum, between its two sclerites.

The postscutellum is represented by a well-marked transverse band behind the scutellum, but not separated from the scutellum by a well-marked suture.

The *metanotum* (Pl. XXX) is like the mesonotum, but with no traces of a præscutum; while the scutellum is much more distinct, diamond-shaped, with distinct sutures, the acute apex not quite reaching the front edge of the scutum; behind clearly demarked from the postscutellum, which forms a definite transverse band.

Pleurum.

The pleurites are very hard to make out, owing to the flatness of the body.

Propleurum. (Pl. XXIX). The episternum is divided into three pieces, the anterior a ridge extending from the sternum to the roof of the scutum; the hinder two a lower piece resting on the trochantine, and an upper, larger and completely chitinous piece extended to the suture. The epimerum is a very irregular, oblong region, partly membranous.

Mesopleurum. (Pl. XXXI.) The episternum in this arthromere is also subdivided into three pieces: the anterior (1) broad and resting on the sternum and reaching around to the epimerum; and (2) a narrow, lanceolate-oval piece not visible from the side; the third sclerite (3) is a broad, triangular piece (which may be the epimerum, but is probably not). A deep fissure seems to separato the episternal from the epimeral area, and the epimerum rests above the trochantine, being minute, rudimentary, and triangular in outline. The coxa is very large, broad, enormous compared with other Orthoptera; it is much flattened. The trochantino is long and narrow, the suture being on a thin, prominent ridge.

Metapleurum. (Pl. XXXI.) Exactly repeats the mesopleurum in form, but is a little larger, and the coxæ are somewhat larger.

Owing to the much depressed, flattened body, which is correlated to the habit of living under the bark of trees and in cracks, the episterna are only seen from beneath, on each side of the sternum, and the epimera are reduced nearly to a minimum, while the coxæ are enormous, but still flattened, as the Blattariæ are active runners rather than leapers.

Sternum.

The *prosternum* (Pl. XXXI) is well developed, but one-half as broad as long, and submembranous.

The *mesosternum* (Pl. XXXII) is about as broad as long, rounded behind, with a median angular depression.

The *metasternum* (Pl. XXXII) is broader than long, deeply cleft, with a median fold or gore. Owing to this deep, angular depression both the meso- and metasternites can be flexed together, thus allowing the sides of the body to approach each other somewhat.

THE ABDOMEN.

There are in the ♀ eight abdominal tergites, the eighth tergito being deeply cleft, and seven urosternites. The cercopoda are short and 13–15 jointed.

NOTE.—The close relation to Termes and the Termitidæ in general, (a point in which, among other respects, Blatta connects the Orthoptera and Pseudoneuroptera), is seen in the nearly identical form of the episternal and epimeral regions; the latter being dorsal and small, the episternal more developed and sternal in position. The sternal region is much the same in Blatta as in Termes, and judging by the form of the head, thorax and abdomen, these two genera might belong to even the same family. They seem certainly only one family removed, the principal differences being in the wings. If there were, so to speak, no other Orthoptera in existence, the Blattariæ would certainly be associated with the Pseudoneuroptera. Hence we have been almost led to think that it is an artificial classification which places them in separate orders.

MANTIDÆ.

THE HEAD.

Mantis carolina. The position of the head is vertical; the front is broad, triangular. The orbits are very large and broad. The epicra-

nium is divided into an occipito-vertical, square area extending from
the occipital foramen and bending over to the ocelli, with a transverse
straight suture or impressed line in front extending to the orbits. The
clypeus is very distinctly divided into a post- and anteclypeus, the
former wider than the anterior division. The labrum is as long as broad
and somewhat pointed in front. The genæ are broad, with a marked
genal ridge. No gular region in front of the foramen. There is no submentum; the montum is square, the ligula small and narrow.

THE THORAX.

The thorax, as well as the rest of the body in general, approaches
that of Blatta, with, of course, important modifications; in some respects
it approaches the Acrydii.

Notum.

The *pronotum* (Pl. XXXIII, figs. 1–3) is remarkably long, forming the
tergal and lateral portions of the area. On the anterior fourth is a
transverse, impressed line, not, however, quite reaching the sides of the
notum; this is situated directly over the insertion of the first pair of
legs.

Mesonotum. (Fig. 4, 5.) This is very long, being about twice as long
as broad; along the middle extends a sclerite from the anterior to the
posterior margin; it is triangular in front and behind; the anterior end
we would regard as the præscutum, and the posterior portion as the
scutellum, the two uniting on the anterior part of the notum. There is
no postscutellum developed. (This union of the præscutum and scutellum is unique in Phyloptera and Neuroptera, but there is an approach
to it in Blatta.)

On each side of the front of the notum, and in front of the insertion
of the wings, is a distinct, triangular sclerite, the nature of which is uncertain.

The scutum is separated into two long halves.

Metanotum. (Fig. 4, 5.) This is a little longer and slightly narrower
posteriorly than the mesonotum, as the hind wings are nearly twice as
wide as the anterior pair.

The præscutum is very distinct, narrow, triangular, truncate at the
apex. The scutellum is very long and narrow, ending in a long, very
acute point before reaching the præscutum; thus the scutum is divided
into two long halves, connected by a very narrow bridge, situated between the præscutum and scutellum, while the mesoscutum is entirely
divided. The postscutellum is obsolete.

Pleurum.

Propleurites. (Fig. 1–3.) The episternum and epimerum are very
small, short, rudimentary, and situated on the anterior fourth of the
prothorax.

The *mesopleurites* (Fig. —) are very oblique. The episternum is divided into two sclerites, the upper one-third as long as the lower and scale-like; the lower oblong, narrow, very long, and on the sternal margin bent down next to the sternite. The epimerum is divided into a long, narrow, linear, chitinous portion next to the episternum, the posterior portion lying in front of the metathorax.

Between the lower end of the episternum and coxa is a small, triangular sclerite which I suppose is the trochantine. The coxa is very large, long and quadrangular.

Metapleurites as the mesopleurites, but the sub-episternum is a little wider, and the sur-episternum is longer, while the epimerum is almost wholly membranous. The trochantine? is more distinct than in the mesothorax. The coxa is of the same form as in mesothorax, but a little thicker.

Sternum.

The *prosternum* (Figs. 1–3) is divided into a præ- and poststernite, the latter remarkably long.

The *mesosternum* is narrow, triangular, flat; the apex bordered on each side with a lateral sternal fold of the integument.

Metasternum. A large part of the sternal surface is occupied by the sternal portions of the episterna, which are bent beneath the body. The sternal area is broader and longer than in the mesosternum, but the limits of the sternite itself are less definite; it appears to be a long, narrow, lanceolate-oval area (but this part needs further comparative study, with more material in species than we possess).

THE ABDOMEN.

There are ten segments or uromeres, with ten tergites. The cercopoda arise from the tenth segment. They are stout, many-jointed, and much as in Blatta, only longer. There are but six urosternites. The eight pairs of stigmata are situated on the membranous pleurites.

Remarks. Mantis is a genuine Orthopter in venation as well as in the fundamental structure of the body, and is truly intermediate in its structure between the Acrydii and the Blattariæ, approximating the latter in the structure of the head, mouth-parts, prothorax, the shape of the abdomen, and its appendages. Blatta, in part, may be regarded as the ancestral or stem form of the Orthoptera, from which all the other Orthoptera may have descended; and this accords in the main with the geological succession of the different Orthopterous families so far as we know it.

PHASMIDA.

THE HEAD.

Diapheromera femoratum. Pupa. The head (Pl. XXV, XXVI) is small, narrow, nearly horizontal, subcylindrical. The epicranium is much developed posteriorly towards the occipital region, being reduced to a minimum in front of the antennæ. The clypeus is very short, undivided, and the labrum is deeply cleft. There is no genal ridge. The gula is rather broad. The submentum and mentum are rather small and narrow.

THE THORAX.

Notum.

The *pronotum* (Pl. XXVIII) is oblong, quadrangular, about twice as long as broad.

The *mesonotum* (Pl. XXX) and *metanotum* are remarkably long and slender, the mesothorax being a little longer than the metathorax, and not differentiated, owing to the want of wings.

Pleurum.

The *propleurum*. (Pl. XXIX.) There are three sclerites on the sides— minute, short, and rudimentary; the anterior is the episternum; the middle the epimerum; and the third and hindermost is the peritreme, bearing the first thoracic stigma; the second pair of stigmata being at the end of the mesopleurum. The coxa is large, cylindrical (a vertical suture along the outer side shows that it is made up of the coxa and trochautine ?).

The *mesopleurum* (Pl. XXXI) is as in the propleurum, but the episternum, as we are disposed to regard it, is larger and extends along, forming a long, very narrow lateral strip, reaching to the prothorax.

The *metapleurum* (Pl. XXXI) exactly repeats the form of the mesopleurum, the episternum in front being somewhat narrower and ending at the mesostigma.

Sternum.

The *prosternum* (Pl. XXXI) is subscutellate, rapidly narrowing in front of the insertion of the legs.

The *mesosternum* (Pl. XXXII) is very long, with a separate piece which we may call the *præsternite*, and which is narrow and crescent-shaped.

The *metasternum* (Pl. XXXII) is as in the mesosternum, but the præsternite is much smaller.

THE ABDOMEN.

There are ten tergites and a rudimentary eleventh. There are nine urosternites. The pleurites are more developed in the ♀ than in the ♂.

THE HEAD.

Prisopus.[181] (Plate XXXIII, figs. 6-9.) The head is as in Diapheromera; the epicranium and clypeus are as described under that genus, but the labrum is less deeply cleft.

---

[181] A common Brazilian species.

THE THORAX.

Notum.

The *pronotum* (Pl. XXXIII, fig. 6) is one-third longer than wide.

The *mesonotum* (Fig. 7) is very long, though shorter than in Diaphero-mera. It is entire, with no signs of subdivision into the scutum, scutel-lum, &c. The presence of the small, net-veined, rudimentary fore wings has not affected or produced a differentiation of the notum, the insertion of the wings being very slightly marked.

In the *metanotum*, owing to the long, large hind wings, with well developed muscular attachments, the notum is differentiated into two lateral swellings, which correspond to two halves of a scutum; while the scutellum is represented by a long, moderately broad area, rounded in front, and at the posterior end narrowed, and with a flattened, boss-like swelling. The scutellum is about one-half as wide as the entire notum, and on the sides it is not definitely separated from the sides of the notum. The hind edge of the notum is emarginate, forming a distinct, rather full ridge extending across the notum. This may repre-sent the postscutellum; but most probably the next sclerite, which I at first took to be the first abdominal segment, is the postscutellum, as the next sclerite bears the first pair of spiracles.

Pleurum.

The pleurites are very much as described in Diapheromera, but the large, long episterna are shorter and broader than in Diapheromera, corresponding with the shorter and thicker proportions of the thorax.

Sternum.

The *prosternum* consists of two sclerites, as in Diapheromera. The *mesosternum* is shorter and broader, but otherwise exactly as in Diaphe-romera. The *metasternum* is much wider than in Diapheromera, with a narrow, intercoxal oblong area, as in Acrydii.

THE ABDOMEN.

The abdomen repeats that of Diapheromera; counting out the very large meta-postscutellum, there are eleven tergites and eight uroster-nites. The cercopoda are jointed, short, much as in Mantis.

NOTE.—This genus connects the Phasmida with the Acrydii, Proscopia being the connecting link in the latter family.

Family ACRYDII.

THE HEAD.

Caloptenus spretus. The head, as in the other genera of Acrydii, is compressed so that the front is high and narrow. No signs of an occip-ital sclerite. In the epicranium the vertex, genæ, and clypeus are well developed. The epicranium extends below the middle of the front, but

not so far down as usual in the other Orthopterous families, though in
Tettix it does extend down much farther than in Caloptenus. The
clypeus is well marked, one-third as long as broad. The genæ are not
very broad; the gula is short and broad.

THE THORAX.

Notum.

The *pronotum* (Pl. XXVIII) is very large, extending to the hinder
edge of the mesonotum, and down on the sides as far as the insertion of
the legs.

The *mesonotum.* (Pl. XXX.) This and the metanotum, except in the
absence of the præscutum, closely resemble the same parts in the Perlidæ. The scutum is short and broad, excavated in front, one-half as
long in the middle as on the sides, each side swollen in the middle area,
the hind edge deeply excavated to receive the scutellum, which is
shorter than wide, obtuse, rounded in front, and behind is a little more
pointed. The postscutellum is represented by a narrow, transverse ridge
expanding on the sides.

The *metanotum* (Pl. XXX) is as the mesonotum, but a little longer, as
the hind wings are larger than the fore pair. The scutellum, with the
sutures separating it in front from the scutum, is more distinct; the scutum is a little longer on the median line; the scutellum is rather more
acute, triangular in front, and longer and larger than the mesoscutellum. The postscutellum is represented by a simple ridge as in the
mesothorax.

Pleurum.

The *propleurum.* (Pl. XXIX.) The episternum is rudimentary,
minute, shorter than broad, and triangular. The epimerum is almost
obsolete, being represented by a short, ridge-like sclerite. The trochantine is rudimentary, minute, with a large spine. The coxa is a little
larger and more swollen sclerite than the trochantine, and is full behind.[182]

The *mesopleurum.* (Pl. XXXI.) The episternum is entire, very large
and full, narrowing towards the insertion of the wings, and extending
below to beneath the insertion of the legs. The epimerum is of even
width, being quite regularly oblong, and only extending to the insertion
of the legs above. The meta-spiracle is situated on the posterior, lower
angle of the epimerum, while the meso-spiracle is placed on the anterior
and upper edge of the episternum. The trochantine and coxa are much
as in the fore legs.

The *metapleurum.* (Pl. XXXI). Much as in the mesopleurum, but
more oblique, and on the whole slightly larger, as the hind wings are
larger. The episternum is narrower below, and much more definitely

[182] In Fig. 13, p. 259 of the 1st Report of the Commission, these parts are wrongly named; the trochantine is the anterior and the coxa is the posterior piece.

separated by an oblique suture from the sternum. The epimerum is less regular in shape than in the mesopleurum, and is more oblique and a little curved. The trochantines are large and longer than those of the two anterior pair of limbs. The coxæ are but slightly developed. The trochantor is oblong, though longer than thick.

In the Orthoptera genuina, Blatta excepted, the trochantines and coxæ are very small, owing to the large pleura and sterna.

Sternum.

The *prosternum* (Pl. XXXI) is short in front, small, broad, triangular, with a scutellate expansion between the coxæ, and a central, long, acute conical tubercle; behind, the sternum expands on each side behind the legs, and is on the same plane as the mesosternum, but separated from it by a well-defined suture; it extends far up on each side of the thorax.

The *mesosternum* (Pl. XXXII) is not so long as broad, but is large, not extending up above the insertion of the middle pair of legs; the surface is a little convex; the hinder edge is excavated, a square portion of the metasternum being dovetailed into it.

The *metasternum* (Pl. XXXII) is wider and longer than the mesosternum, the sides extending up the thorax. The sternum is divided into four parts by sutures; the anterior part has just been described, the posterior is a piece nearly as long and a little wider than the first urosternite, and sends a square portion corresponding to, but smaller than, the one on the mesosternum into the latter sclerite; the two lateral narrow parts lie next to the coxæ.

THE ABDOMEN.

There are ten uromeres (Pl. XXXIV–XXXVIII), represented by ten tergites, and seven urosternites; no pleurites are developed, the eight pairs of spiracles opening on the lower edge of the tergites. The tenth tergite is telson-like, with a triangular pleurite, on each side bearing the cercopoda, which are not jointed. The tenth tergite extends beyond the base of the upper pair of rhabdites.

PROSCOPIA.

THE HEAD.

The high, vertical prolongation of the head in this remarkable insect is a development of the epicranium; the occipital region of the epicranium is also greatly produced, carrying the eyes and insertion of the antennæ much beyond the middle of the head; the space between the eyes is very narrow. The singular, four-angled process projecting above the insertion of the antennæ arises from the vertical rather than from the frontal region of the epicranium, as there is a long space between the insertion of the antennæ and eyes and the clypeus. The latter is very short and divided into post, and anteclypeus, though the two divisions are not separated by a distinct suture. The labrum is deeply hollowed out in front.

THE THORAX.

Notum.

Pronotum. (Pl. XXVIII.) The prothorax is remarkably long, cylindrical, and full in the middle. It is very singular for having no sternum as distinguished from the tergum, but the segment is perfectly cylindrical, with only a fine, lateral, straight suture, which is obsolete behind the legs; while along the sternal region behind the legs there is a median, fine suture. The episternum is present, but no epimerum is differentiated from the tergum. The anterior spiracles are situated on the front edge of the mesothorax, and these are really the usual prothoracic ones, while there is another pair on the hind edge of the mesothorax on the rudimentary mesepimerum.

The *mesonotum* (Pl. XXX) consists of a single oblong sclerite, one third longer than broad, very slightly separated from the pleurum; the surface is rounded and rough like the rest of the segment.

The *metanotum* (Pl. XXX) consists of two portions which have no resemblance to a scutum and scutellum, but which are separated on the side by a diverging ridge extending down the sides into the epimerum; the anterior area is short, transversely broad, while the posterior area is not separated by suture from the anterior, but is as long as broad, and rounded in front. It is interesting to notice the extreme modification of the meso- and metanotum, owing to the absence of wings, and also those characteristics due to the cylindrical form of the body. Proscopia is a link between the Acrydii and the Phasmida.

Pleurum.

The *mesopleurites* (Pl. XXXI) are well marked sclerites, but are still subordinated in form and relation to the cylindrical form of the body. They are oblique, separated by a fine suture from the tergum. The episternum is large and broad, irregular in shape, while the epimerum is much shorter, and not much longer than wide. The pro-peritremes, bearing the prostigmata, are separated by suture from the prothorax, and the meso-peritreme is consolidated with the posterior edge of the mesepimerum.

The *metapleurites* (Pl. XXXI) are much as in the mesothorax, but shorter. The episternum is straight-edged; though oblique in its general position, it is as wide as in the mesothorax, while the epimerum is less than half as wide as the mesepimerum, and the upper portion is reduced to a mere ridge, which extends upon the notum. The metacoxæ are as in Diapheromera, being twice as large as those of the mesothoracic segment, while the procoxæ are a little smaller than those of the metathorax.

Sternum.

The *sternites* (Pl. XXXII) are broad pieces, the meso- and metasternites not separated by suture. The external openings of the mes-entothorax and met-entothorax are conspicuous and situated between the second and third pair of legs.

Conocephalus. In the head of this genus the entire epicranium is produced tergally into a long cone, with no suture above. Beneath, there is a deep inter-antennal fossa dividing the cone from the face, which is longer than broad. There are no ocelli. There is no suture between the clypeus and epicranium, except on the sides.

Family LOCUSTARIÆ.

THE HEAD.

Anabrus. (Pl. XXV–XXVI). The epicranium is very large, and divided into two portions, post- and ante-antennal, which are separated by a short interantennal suture. The front of the head is very broad, and the eyes are small. There is an occipital ridge on the hinder edge, separating the genæ from the ocular region. The clypeus is trapezoidal, about one-half as long as wide, with an accessory, rounded, anterior expansion on the base of the labrum; the latter rounded, as long as broad. The genæ are broad and flat; the gula moderately broad.

THE THORAX.

Notum.

The *pronotum* (Pl. XXVIII) is very large, extending down to the insertion of the fore legs and backward to the base of the abdomen.

Mesonotum. (Pl. XXX.) The scutum and scutellum are only partially differentiated, the scutal area being represented by two lateral, flattened, slightly-marked bosses on each side of the segment in front, and not separated by suture from the scutellum, whose apex is distinct and acute. There is no præscutum or postscutellum.

The *metanotum* (Pl. XXX) repeats the general features of the mesonotum, but the segment is a little shorter, the scutal bosses smaller, while the scutellum is indicated by a circular, flattened eminence, with no apex behind. The postscutellum is not indicated.

Pleurum.

The *propleurites* (Pl. XXIX) are small and short. There are two episternal sclerites, an upper and lower, of irregular form. The epimerum is undivided; it is no longer than broad, and below laterally flares outward, forming a horizontally-projecting scale. The prostigmata are very large, and the edges are armed within by thick-set spines.

The *mesopleurites* and *metapleurites* are much alike and peculiar in form, being large and high, owing to the small wings. The episternum is long and narrow, and vertical in position; it is undivided, and a little narrower above than near the sternum, the middle being produced into a sharp ridge. The epimerum is as in the episternum, but flatter and only ridged near the sternum.

The *metapleurites* are more oblique than the mesopleurites, and are a little longer and larger, the entire segment being a little larger than the mesothorax. The coxæ are stout and thick; those of the prothorax spined.

Sternum.

The sternites (Pl. XXXI, XXXII) are peculiar in this genus and family. The *prosternum* is very short and broad; the coxæ are situated rather far apart. The *mesosternum* is divided into two portions; the anterior (præsternite) is divided by a median sinus into two lateral swollen areas, while behind, at the base of each coxa, is a stout, triangular spine.

In the *metasternum* the anterior sternal portion or præsternite merely forms a transverse, curvilinear ridge, from each side of which arises a stouter posterior spine than in the mesosternum.

THE ABDOMEN.

There are ten and perhaps eleven uromeres; nine large square tergites and a tenth narrower one, the tenth segment bearing the small unjointed cercopoda. The supra-anal plate probably represents the eleventh tergite, but it is not separated very distinctly by suture from the tenth uromere. The pleurites are broad but membranous. There are eight pairs of abdominal stigmata, which are situated on the pleurum. Of the sternites, the first seven are small and narrow, surrounded by membrane; the eighth is large and square. The ovipositor is enormous. (The proportion of parts in Phaneroptera is seen in Plates XXXIV–XXXVIII.)

Family GRYLLIDÆ.

THE HEAD.

Gryllus neglectus. The head is rounded, full, vertical in position, smooth, with no areas, although the three ocelli are present. The clypeus is separated by suture from the epicranium; it is divided into two parts, the post-clypeus being short and very broad, and separated on the sides by a well-marked suture from the ante-clypeus, which is considerably shorter and not so wide as the labrum, the latter being one-half as long as broad. The genal ridges are remote and posterior to the orbits. The gular region is unusually broad; the mentum is much shorter and smaller than the submentum.

THE THORAX.

Notum.

Pronotum is broad and flat, square, nearly as long as broad, and bent over the sides, so that the pleurites are very short; posteriorly it overlaps the mesonotum.

Mesonotum is very simple in structure. It is very short, being one-third as long as the pronotum and also one-third as long as the metanotum; the scutum is very short, consisting of two lateral raised areas, nearly separated by the large, broad, swollen scutellum, the latter transversely lozenge-shaped, being rounded in front and a little more angular behind.

Metanotum. On the same plan as the mesonotum, but about three times as long; the scutum is very short and slightly depressed in the middle, enlarging and swollen on the sides. The scutellum is of the same shape as in the mesonotum, but much larger; behind it is a moderately broad, flat band, representing the postscutellum.

Pleurum.

Propleurum. In the prothorax the episternum is represented by two small sclerites, one forming a spine. The epimerum is minute, rudimentary, submembranous. The coxa and trochantine are consolidated into a single, large, thick coxal joint. The prostigmata are rather large and situated on a distinct peritreme.

Mesopleurum. The episternum is divided into three sclerites, the upper much larger than the two lower sclerites, and triangular, with the apex produced towards the insertion of the wings, but not extending up so high as the epimerum. Of the two other sclerites one is supracoxal, and the other is next to the sternum. The epimerum is a large, lanceolate-oval, scale-like, single sclerite, with the posterior edge free, below which is the mesostigma.

Metapleurum. This is much larger than the pleurum of the meso-thorax. The episternum is large, oblique, narrow triangular, with the apex extending as far as the upper end of the epimerum; the latter is quite wide, narrowing below; the hind margin is not, however, free.

Sternum.

Prosternum. This is in part rudimentary, and consists of a transverse row of three small sclerites surrounded by membrane, behind which are two larger sclerites, and above, on each side, is a subtriangular piece. Between the coxæ, which are wide apart, is a small, triangular sternite, which sends off long, chitinous angles towards the episternal spines. Behind this is a narrow, long, scutel-like sclerite.

Meso- and metasternum. These are both large, broad, solid sclerites, as long as broad, angulated obtusely on the sides, and notched in the middle of the posterior margin, especially on the metathorax.

THE ABDOMEN.

There are eleven uromeres: eleven tergites, the 11th being the supra-anal plate; the 10th is narrower than the 9th, and situated between the cercopoda, which are large and long and obscurely jointed. The 11th tergite is separated by a faint suture from the 10th tergite. The pleural region is rather broad, bearing the eight pairs of stigmata. There are eight well-developed urosternites; the 7th is twice as long as the basal seven. The 8th is small and rounded behind.

THE HEAD.

Gryllotalpa borealis. The head and prothorax are admirably adapted to the fossorial habits of this insect. The head is long, and rounded above. The clypeus is very short, the postclypeus less than one-half as long as the anteclypeus. The labrum is long and narrow. The gular region is broad, the genæ small.

THE THORAX.

Notum.

Pronotum. This part is immensely developed, being equal in bulk to the rest of the thorax.

Mesonotum. This is remarkably short, not quite so long as broad, and about one-half as long as the metanotum. There is no præscutum. The scutum is, along the median line, shorter than the scutellum, and is excavated behind in the middle to receive the scutellum, which is rather large and broader than long. There is no postscutellum.

Metanotum. More than twice as long as the mesonotum. The scutum is as long as broad, with a boss on each side above, and a posterior, rather flat area, succeeded by the scutellum, which is broader than long.

Pleurum.

Propleurum. This is represented by an irregularly triangular sclerite, whose apex below bears a stout, downward-projecting spine. The coxa is very thick and rather large, and excavated in front to receive the posterior prolongation of the base of the femur, which is remarkably short, thick, large, and broad, as is the tibia, this and the tarsi being described by other authors.

Mesopleurum. The episternum and epimerum are moderate in width, and oblong; the episternum is broader than the epimerum, and the sclerites are placed vertically and not obliquely.

Metapleurum. The sclerites are large and broad, the sides of this segment being square and vertical, though the sclerites themselves are obliquely situated. The episternum is one large piece resting below on the sternum; the epimerum is as long as the episternum, but narrower. The hinder coxæ are less spherical and swollen than the mesocoxæ.

Sternum.

The *prosternum* is obsolete, being reduced to a narrow membrane situated between the coxæ, which closely meet.

The *mesosternum* is very large and broad, with a curvilinear impressed line between the coxæ.

THE ABDOMEN.

There are ten uromeres; ten tergites, the tenth rudimentary, triangular, short. There are nine urosternites. The pleural ridge is well developed. The cercopoda are long and filamental, thick at base, multiarticulate.

There are no prothoracic stigmata, but the first pair is situated on the back of the mesothorax behind the coxæ; and the second pair on the metathorax behind the epimera and above the coxæ. I can discover only seven pairs of abdominal spiracles.

21 E O

THE HEAD.

Œcanthus niveus ♀.—The head is long and narrow. The suture between the post- and anteclypeus is obsolete in the middle. The occipital and gular regions are much developed, while the genæ are narrow.

THE THORAX.

Notum.

The *pronotum* is long and narrow.

The *mesonotum* is very short; the scutum almost wanting, very short, while the scutellum is about one-third as long as wide.

The *metanotum* is a little longer than wide; the scutum is shorter than broad, slightly swollen on each side; the scutellum is one-half as long as the scutum, unusually broad, regularly convex, very obtusely angular behind, succeeded by a thin, transverse ridge, which is perhaps the postscutellum.

Pleurum.

The *propleurum* is minute and rudimentary.

The *mesopleurum* is very short and oblique; the episternum is a long oblong sclerite which is moderately broad, while the epimerum is very narrow, but as long as the episternum.

The *metapleurum* is also very oblique, but the two sclerites are of the same width, and both are somewhat broader and larger than the mesepisterna.

Sternum.

All the sternites are broad and full, as indicated in Fig.   , so that the coxæ are wide apart.

THE ABDOMEN.

There are eleven uromeres; eleven tergites, and eight urosternites. The cercopoda are long, multiarticulate, while the ovipositor is large, long, and well developed.

Remarks.—This family is evidently closely allied to the Locustariæ, while the Acrydii and Phasmida are closely allied, the Mantidæ standing below next to the lowest group, the Blattariæ.

Order IV. PSEUDONEUROPTERA.

Suborder 1. CORRODENTIA.

PERLIDÆ. Plates XL, XLIV, LVII.

THE HEAD.

Pteronarcys californica. (Pl. XL, figs. 1–2.) No occiput. Epicranium divided into three regions; vertex large and well marked, about one-fourth as long as broad; eyes on each side; no orbits; the ocellar area separated from the vertex by a well-marked suture, broad, somewhat V-shaped. Separated from the third area in front by a deeply-impressed line.

Clypeus narrow, one-half as long as wide, with a narrow projection in front. Labrum small, narrow, short, and partly fleshy. Genæ ·of moderate extent. Gula but slightly developed; mentum short, distinct from the submentum.

THE THORAX.

Notum.

Pronotum (Pteronarcys californica). (Pl. LVII, fig. 1.) Broad and Square, nearly as long as broad.

Mesonotum (Pteronarcys californica). (Fig. 2.) Præscutum sub-cordate, rhomboidal, with the posterior half triangular, divided by a deep mesial impressed line; anterior half smooth and swollen. Patagia (?) large and broad.

Scutum very peculiar. It is broader than long, with two large lateral bosses in front, apparently corresponding to the two halves of the scutum in the Neuroptera metamorphotica, and between them is a broad, slightly convex area, which might be regarded as the anterior part of the scutellum, but judging by the limits of the metascutellum it is not.

Scutellum short and broad, well marked behind, but in front insensibly merging into the central flat area of the scutum, with no indications of a suture.

Postscutellum, forming a transverse linear ridge of even width throughout, with very slight indications of an impressed line along the middle of the body.

Metanotum. (Fig. 3.) Exactly repeats the form of the mesonotum, and is, if anything, a little longer than the mesonotum (the hind wings being considerably larger). Only the posterior half of the præscutum in the mesonotum is represented in the metanotum, *i. e.*, the cordate, roughened portion, with the mesial suture. The lateral bosses of the scutum are as far asunder as in the mesonotum. Scutellum crescent-shaped; the suture in front is distinct, whereas in the mesonotum it is obsolete.[155]

Postscutellum a little larger behind the scutellum than in the mesonotum.

Behind the metapostscutellum is a long, transverse, rather broad membrane which connects the metanotum with the abdomen. It is not the first abdominal segment.

Pleurum.

Propleurum (Pteronarcys californica). (Pl. XLIV, Fig. 1.) Episternum and epimerum both nearly equally developed; the former subtriangular, the latter subquadrate, and each in part semi-membranous.

---

[155] In *Acroneuria abnormis* the meso- and metascutellum are not separated by suture from the scutum.

Mesopleurum. (Fig. 2.) The flanks are obliquely inclined. The epi-sternum is divided into a supra-episternite and an infra-episternite; the latter is trapezoidal, a little longer than broad, with a broad projection extending round in front, resting upon the mesosternum. The supra-episternite is sub-diamond-shaped, the lower edge triangular, fitting into the infra episternite.

The epimerum is divided into two pieces; the infra-epimerite is nearly as broad as long; the sub-epimerite is long, oblique, irregular in form, with three large projections from the surface.

Trochantine broad and short. Coxa small compared with the troch-antine, being about one-third as large.

Metapleurum. (Fig. 3.) Exactly repeats the structure of the meso‚ pleurum, except that it is a little longer, as the hind wings are larger than the anterior pair. Coxa and trochantine the same as in the meso-thorax.

Sternum.

Prosternum (Pteronarcys californica). (Fig. 4.) Represented only by a swollen fold in front of the insertions of the legs. and by a gill-bearing membranous swelling behind. In *Acroneuria abnormis* there is a broad, large, scutellate chitinous piece.

Mesosternum (Pt. californica). (Fig. 5.) This sternite consists of two portions, (1) a raised, rounded sclerite (præsternite) longer than broad, and situated on the front of the sternal area, between the two anterior gills; (2) behind is the true sternum, which is a very broad, trans-versely-oblong sclerite, square on the sides, and about one-fourth as long as broad, and somewhat curvilinear. In *Acroneuria abnormis* the mesosternum is divided into (1) a large præsternite, which is broad and triangular; and (2) a large trapezoidal sternite.

Metasternum. (Fig. 6.) The same as in the mesothorax, but slightly larger. Behind the sternite, on both meso- and metathorax, are in each segment two deep fossæ, extending probably into the entothorax (medi-and postfurea). In *Acroneuria* the metasternum is the same in form as the mesosternum, but the *præsternite* is shorter and broader.

THE UROSOME (ABDOMEN).

In *Pteronarcys californica* (Pl. XLIV, figs. 7-9) there are ten abdominal segments (uromeres). The tergites are ten in number, the first broad and well developed, the tenth small and very short, with a median tri-angular projection (supraanal plate); the segment is entire but very short sternally. There. are no pleurites, except nearly obsolete mem-branous folds on the first and second uromeres, on which the first and second pair of spiracles are situated; on the other uromeres the remain-ing six pair are situated on the lower edge of the tergites. From the hinder edge of the eighth urosternite two short, stout spines project backwards. From the tenth urosome apair of long, multiarticulate cercopoda arise from broad basal joints or flaps, forming lateral anal plates.

PSOCIDÆ. Plate XXXIX, XLIII.

THE HEAD.

Psocus novæ-scotiæ.[184] (Pl. XXXIX, figs. 6–8.) The head is in its structure allied to that of the Perlidæ. Epicranium horizontal, nearly as long as broad, being square on the sides. Ocelli situated close together between the eyes. Clypeus very large and swollen, situated between the antennæ; in front is a semi-membranous division, which may be the ante-clypeus; this sclerite is not quite so wide as the large, broad labrum. The gular region and mentum are broad.

THE THORAX.

Notum.

Pronotum (*Psocus novæ-scotiæ* Walk). Very small, depressed, overlapped by the heade, bing much reduced in size compared with the Perlidæ.

Mesonotum (Pl. XLIII, fig. 10) very high and convex; seen from above, much rounded in front. Præscutum large, prominent, high and rounded, subcordate, but with no median impressed line.

Scutum very short and broad, deeply excavated in front for the reception of the præscutum; each side is much swollen, the swollen areas being separated by the broad median impressed line.

Scutellum small and short, three or four times as wide as long, with a median acute angle in front, and angulated on each side anteriorly; while from each posterior angle a high narrow ridge diverges to the hinder part of the insertion of the fore wing. No postscutellum is visible.

Metanotum (Fig. 11) small, one-half as long as the mesonotum. The præscutum is very small, subtriangular, broad and short, depressed. Scutum one-quarter as long as broad, consisting of two inflated halves, with a median impressed line.

Scutellum minute, rudimentary, somewhat rounded.

Pleurum.

Propleurum. The episternum and epimerum rudimentary, though rather long; while the coxa and trochantine are large and long, being well developed.

Mesopleurum. (Fig. 12.) Episternum and epimerum long and narrow; not oblique, but vertical; the episternum a little thicker than the epimerum.

---

[184] A large species of Psocus inhabiting coniferous trees in Maine; kindly identified by Dr. Hagen.

Metapleurum.' (Fig. 12.) Episternum much as in mesothorax, but the epimerum is narrow; triangular, and reduced to a point next to the trochantine. Coxa and trochantine well developed, rather long and large; the coxa considerably narrower than the trochantine.

Sternum.

Prosternum. Very small, rudimentary.

Mesosternum very small, triangular; the coxæ nearly meeting on the median line of the body.

Metasternum small.

TERMITIDÆ.   Plates XXXIX, figs. 1–5; XL, figs. 3, 4, 8; XLI, XLII, XLIII, figs. 1–9.

THE HEAD.

Termopsis angusticollis. (Pl. XXXIX, figs. 1–3.) The head is broad and flat, oblong-oval in shape. The epicranial region is remarkably simple, not subdivided, with no V-shaped suture, and the eyes are very small. The clypeus is very simple, very short and broad; and only an impressed line, no suture, separates it from the epicranium. The labrum is large, one-half as long as broad, and much longer than the clypeus. The genæ are separated from the upper portion of the epicranium by a sharp, lateral, conspicuous ridge. The gular region is small, membranous. The labium is not differentiated into a submentum and mentum.

In *Termes flavipes* (figs. 4, 5) the head is oblong, with faint traces of a V-shaped suture; the clypeus is subdivided into an anterior and posterior portion, the two subequal and well marked.

THE THORAX.

Notum.

Pronotum (Termopsis). (Pl. XLIII, fig. 1.) Somewhat crescent-shaped, being excavated in front and rounded behind.

Mesonotum. (Fig. 2.) Remarkably square, as long as broad, with the elements but partly differentiated, an approach to that of Pteronarcys, the slight partial anterior attachment of the wings being correlated with the undeveloped nature of the tergal sclerites. The præsentum is not visible.

The scutellum is not differentiated from the scutum; the latter forming a somewhat swollen flattened boss on each side, but in the middle of the notum contracted, becoming narrow, the region where the scutellum usually is being about a quarter less wide than the scutal region. Postscutellum wanting.

Metanotum. (Fig. 3.) Considerably smaller than the mesonotum, hour-glass shaped, being much contracted in the middle, forming an

anterior or scutal and a posterior or scutellar region. Each side of the
scutal region is swollen in front, but the scutellum is not indicated by
sutures. Posteriorly the scutellar region spreads out laterally. The
wings on both segments are only attached by feeble, local, restricted
areas to the front part of the scutum.

In *Termes flavipes* (Pl. XLII, figs. 1–3) there are important differences
from Termopsis.

The *pronotum* is one-half as long as the head, well rounded behind,
and one-fourth shorter than broad.

In the *mesonotum* the scutum and scutellum are differentiated; the
scutum is broad and short, one-half as long as broad, and rounded behind. The scutellum is quite free from it, and is larger than the scutum,
being longer, with the sides prolonged toward the posterior insertion of
the wings.

In the *metanotum* (Fig. 3) the scutum is very broad and short, shorter
than the mesoscutum, and only two-thirds as long as the metascutellum; the latter is large and broad, being a little shorter than broad.
No præ- or postscutellum in either segment.

The meso- and metanotum are considerably narrower than the thorax
itself, and are margined with membrane, the insertion of the wings
being tergal and very weak.

Pleurum.

Propleurum (*Termopsis angusticollis*). (Fig. 4.) The sides of the prothorax are much flattened, as if (seen from above) the body had been
squeezed and the flanks pressed out, so that they present a rather wide
lateral area on each side of the tergites. The episternum forms a narrow (vertically) linear piece. The epimerum is membranous, narrow,
but wider than the episternum. The coxa and trochantine are consolidated in one large oval-oblong sclerite.

Mesopleurum. (Fig. 5.) Episternum forming one large, irregular
piece, expanding above the middle, anteriorly forming a triangle. The
epimerum is much smaller and semi-membranous. The trochantine is
large and long, being oblong-ovate; coxa as long as the trochantine, but
narrower, and pressed up (so to speak) beyond it.

Metapleurum. (Fig. 6.) Much shorter than that of the mesothorax.
Episternum much narrower, while the trochantine is broader and much
shorter in proportion; otherwise much as in the preceding segment.

In *Termes flavipes* (Fig. 4) the pro-episternum is represented by a
narrow sclerite situated in front of and below the pronotum, and separated from the sternites by a suture. The epimerum is a minute, triangular sclerite situated over the coxa. The trochantine is large and
long, and the coxa is of the same length.

Mesopleurum. (Fig. 5.) The episternum is well developed, narrow,
curved, triangular. The epimerum is much smaller, and both pieces are
situated obliquely. The trochantine and coxa are of the same size and

length, and are unusually free from each other, the two sclerites together forming a very broad and thick portion for the attachment of the legs.

Metapleurum. (Fig. 6.) Much as in the mesopleurum, with the coxa pointed at the lower and posterior end; both the meso- and metapleurites are more oblique than the propleurites, while the meta- are fully as large as the mesopleurites.

Sternum.

Termopsis. (Fig. 7.) The prosternum is triangular, about as long as broad.

The mesosternum is about three times as large as the prosternum, and also equilaterally triangular, with the posterior apex acute. Metasternum?

Termes flavipes. (Figs. 7–9.) The prosternum is rudimentary, consisting of four sclerites; two large ones next to the episternum in front, and two minute triangular ones behind. The meso- and metasterna are entire, broadly triangular, and rather large, with a pair of accessory sclerites in front of the coxæ. The coxæ seen from beneath are divided by a deeply-impressed longitudinal line.

THE ABDOMEN.

The abdomen of *Termopsis* is much as in Blatta; it is very flat, broad, oval-oblong; ten uromeres, the first tergite broad and long; the tenth

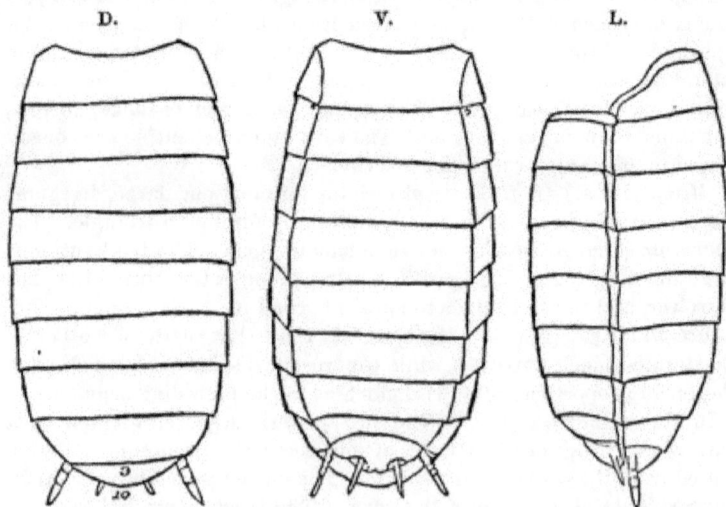

FIG. 12.—Abdomen of Termopsis angusticollis. D, dorsal; V, ventral; L, lateral view. Enlarged. Gissler, del.

short, triangular, small, only extending between the short five-jointed cercopoda. There are nine urosternites. The pleurites of the abdomen (uropleurites) are only seen from beneath, but are well developed. The abdomen of *Termes flavipes* is substantially as in Termopsis.

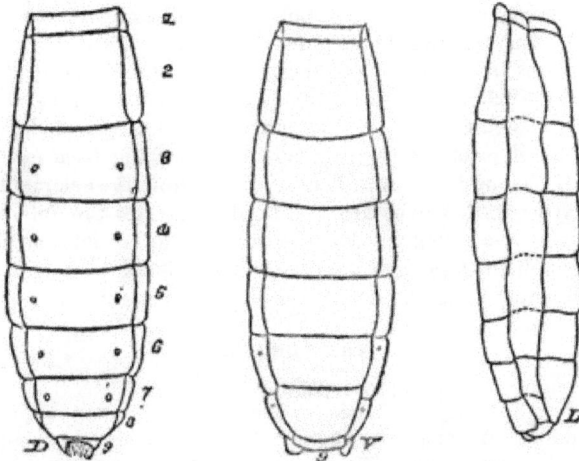

FIG. 13.—Abdomen of Termes flavipes. Lettering as in fig. 12. Enlarged.

Suborder 2. ODONATA. Plates XLVII–L.

THE HEAD.

Agrion verticale Say. (Pl. XLVII, figs. 4–6.) The structure of the head of Agrion and Calopteryx is more easily understood than that of Æschna and Libellula, as their eyes are much smaller, and the development of the epicranium is more equable and normal. The head is unusually short and wide; the orbits very wide; eyes spherical. The epicranium, exclusive of the orbits, is about as long as broad, with a decided ocellar area, the ocelli being large and closely contiguous. In front of the ocelli is a deep impressed line parallel to the clypeus.

The clypeus is moderately large, about one-half as long as broad, with a high, sharp, shelf-like side; it is divided into a clypeus posterior and anterior; the post-clypeus being horizontal like a shelf, and the anteclypeus forming a vertical wall.

The labrum is large and broad, well rounded in front. The genæ are very large and broad, smooth, and continuous with the orbits. The gula is membranous.

In *Calopteryx maculata* the head is much as in Agrion, but the clypeus is more clearly defined and separate from the epicranium than in Agrion. The epicranium is wider and larger than in Agrion; a transverse impressed line separates it into a posterior and anterior area.

In *Æschna heros* (Pl. XLVII, figs. 1–3) there is no definite trace of the occiput, unless a postorbital ridge between the gula and orbits marks its limits. This ridge becomes obsolete towards the median line near the vertex. As the eyes are enormous and meet on the median line of the head, the epicranium is divided by them into three portions: 1, a narrow orbito-gular area, not seen from above; 2, an ocello-antennal, very small, subtriangular area; and 3, a pre-antennal, large area, corresponding to the small ante-antennal area in Agrion. This area, with the clypeus, forms the peculiar shelf-like projection of the front of the head. The area is divided into a horizontal broad area and a transverse crescent-shaped subarea, separated from the horizontal portion by a sharp ridge. The clypeus is very large and full, reaching from eye to eye, and nearly as long as broad. It is separated from the epicranium by a well-marked curvilinear suture. In front it incloses the ante-clypeus, which is a crescent-shaped sclerite no wider than the labrum, and separated by a distinct suture from the clypeus proper.

The labrum is large and broad, very distinct from the clypeus.

THE THORAX.

Notum.

The Odonata are characterized by the unusual development of the pleurites, the meso-episternum forming the larger part of the dorsum of the thorax, the meso- and metanotum being greatly reduced in size, owing to the great and long-sustained powers of flight possessed by these insects.

In Agrion the *pronotum* (Pl. XLVII, fig. 10) is well developed compared with the meso- and metanotum; somewhat broader than long, divided into three areas, being emarginate in front and behind, with the edges turned up, while the large central area has two lateral, slightly swollen areas.

Mesonotum. (Fig. 11.) The præscutum not visible; scutum entire, minute, not much longer than wide. The scutellum is a much swollen rounded knob, with the base subtriangular, not much smaller than the scutum. The post-scutellum appears to be a moderately broad, even, two-ridged, transverse band.

The *metanotum* (Fig. 11) repeats the general appearance of the mesonotum and is of the same size, the wings being alike. The præscutum is not visible. The scutum is deeply divided into two halves, each half minute and much swollen. The scutellum as in mesonotum, but considerably larger. The post-scutellum is very distinct, forming a transversely-oblong piece no wider than the scutellum.

Calopteryx (Pl. XLVIII, figs. 5–6) is substantially as in Agrion, as regards the notum.

In *Æschna heros* the *pronotum* is small and narrow, and nearly concealed from above by the head. It is about two-thirds as long as broad, divided into a short transverse ridge and a posterior, longer portion subtriangular behind, by a deep constriction or impressed line.

Mesonotum. (Pl. XLVIII, fig. 3.) The præscutum obsolete, not visible from above. Scutum subtrapezoidal, longer than broad; acute behind, with an appendicular area between the conical end and the scutellum, consisting of two diverging tubercles, from which a narrow ridge falls away on each side, forming the origin of the 5th vein of the wings on each side. (Fig. 3, v. 5.)

The scutellum is swollen, triangular, as broad as long, the apex directed backwards and wedged in between the separate halves of the post-scutellum, which is represented by two triangular bosses, the apices separated by the pointed end of the scutellum, the bases connected by a ridge concealed by the end of the scutellum.

Metanotum. (Fig. 4.) There is a pair of patagia, one in front of the base of each hind wing. No praescutum. The scutum is much larger than the mesoscutum, a little longer than broad; each side raised into an oblong-oval boss, with a narrow, acute, triangular, depressed, flat area between, and bounded behind by a converging ridge, which is succeeded by a peculiar diverging ridge (v. 5), like that in the mesonotum, which is the origin of the 5th vein of the second pair of wings.

The scutellum is much larger than in the mesonotum, nearly square, smooth and flat; the posterior one-half vertical, thin, and more or less elastic and membranous, moving upon the abdomen. (This posterior portion may represent the post-scutellum, which is otherwise absent, but there are no signs of a suture.) Post-scutellum absent (?) See Fig. 4, p. scl.'', for what may prove to be the post-scutellum.

Pleurum.

In *Agrion* (Fig. 7) the pro-episternum and epimerum of each side are minute, rudimentary, and submembranous, and in position are vertical,

Mesopleurum. The episternum in the Odonata differs remarkably from all other Pseudoneuroptera and indeed from all other insects, only the Acrydii approaching them in the enormously long and large episterna, which meet in front to form a large, dorsal, convex area, that usually occupied in other insects by the scutum. The epimerum is a similar piece, and nearly as large as the lateral portion of the episternum; it is in Agrion consolidated with the meta-episternum. In Calopteryx, however (Fig. 6), where the thorax is broader and higher, the two sclerites are separate.

The coxae are small, conical; the trochantine is small, triangular, and situated directly over the small conical coxa.

Metapleurum. (Fig. 8.) The episternum repeats the form of that of the mesopleurum, but is consolidated with the meso-episternum. The episternum, seen laterally, is regularly oblong, and three times as long as broad.

The trochantine is a triangular piece, situated directly over the small subconical coxa.

In Calopteryx (Fig. 6) the meso-episternum and epimerum are much

as in Agrion; those of the metapleurum are much as in the meso-, but
a well-marked suture separates the meso-epimerum from the meta-episternum, and the latter is much wider towards the insertion of the wing
than next to the coxa.

In the prothorax of Æschna the episternum is very small, and subdivided into several pieces; the epimerum is larger and not divided; it
is about as long as broad, and posteriorly submembranous.

The coxa is very large, being much enlarged within, meeting the
opposite coxa on the median line.

Mesopleurum (Fig. 1) enormous, and forming a large part of the dorsal region of the thorax. The episternum is enormous, forming with
its fellow on the opposite side a large proportion of the front and mesonotum; the foramen leading into the prothorax is situated very low,
the mesostigmata being situated on the upper side of the opening.
The two meso-episterna unite to form the front of the mesothorax and
also the anterior fourth or third of the dorsal region of the entire thorax.
Dorsally there is on the united episterna a high median ridge becoming forked behind, with two lateral diverging transverse ridges. The
ridge originates in front from the hinder border of a transverse crescent-shaped area directly above the foramen leading into the prothorax. A straight, distinct suture separates the episternum from the
epimerum. Between the episternum and the trochantine is a sclerite, the
nature of which is uncertain; by its close relation to the sternum it may
be the infra-episternum and probably not the coxa, the latter appearing
to be obsolete.

The epimerum is large, broad, oblique, and below in front of the metastigma separated by suture from the meta-episternum, but above there
is no suture, only a broad, valley-like depression.

Metapleurum. The episternum is about one-half as wide as the large,
swollen, smooth epimerum, which composes the posterior third of the
pleurum of the thorax. Below the metastigma is a square sclerite,
directly over the trochantine, which is probably the infra-episternum,
there apparently being no coxa; the trochantine as in the prothorax.

Sternum.

In Agrion the prosternum is small, triangular, longer than broad,
with the apex acute.

Mesosternum a little larger and broader than the prosternum, but
still small.

Metasternum. What I am disposed to regard as this sclerite is a very
large, elongated, polygonal area, which is semi-membranous and flat.

In Calopteryx the sternites are as in Agrion, but the metasternum is
broader and shorter, with an anterior deeply impressed median line.

In Æschna the mesosternum is small, broad, irregular; while the
metasternum is much smaller, nearly obsolete in front of the legs,

and behind is a broad, sternal, large area, broader and shorter than in
Agrion.

It should be observed that in Odonata the middle and hind legs are
close together.

THE ABDOMEN.

In *Agrion* (Pl. L, figs. 4–6) there are ten uromeres. The first tergite is
well-developed, the second one-half as long as the five succeeding tergites.
No pleurites, the tergites overlapping the urosternites, which are very
narrow. The tenth urosome shorter than broad. The claspers possibly
represent an eleventh urosome, as such a segment is developed in the
embryo, but in the adult the claspers appear to be appendages (cercopoda) of the tenth urosome. Calopteryx closely resembles Agrion as
to its abdomen.

In *Æschna* (Pl. XLIX, L. figs. 1–3) there are ten uromeres; and the
rudiments of an eleventh urosternite; the cercopoda (c) are long and
spatulate.

Suborder 3 EPHEMERINA. Plates XLV, XLVI.

THE HEAD.

Ephemera.—It has been difficult with the material at my command to
properly describe the external anatomy of any member of this group.
The species examined was our commonest Ephemera in Rhode Island,
identified by Dr. Hagen as probably *E. cupida* (Leptophlebia) Walk.,
and also a species of Palingenia. There is a great deal of variation in
the form of the thorax and head in the genera of this suborder, which
is as much specialized in its way as the Odonata is in its.

In examining the under side of the head of an alcoholic Ephemera,
the subject of the drawing made by Dr. Gissler (Fig. 2), there is a cav-
ernous area, at the bottom of which I can discover what appear to be
the rudiments of the maxillæ and labium. There are certainly no rudiments of the mandibles. The gular region and the mentum can be distinguished, and I think I can detect the labial palpi and lingua; con-
cerning the maxillæ I am less certain. The drawing was made by Dr.
Gissler from but one specimen, and while correct in most respects he
regards the sketch of the mouth-parts as provisional. The general
relations of the under side of the head are as he drew them, with one or
two corrections made by the writer.

In an alcoholic specimen of *Palingenia bilineata* (perhaps a subimago)
I can discover no certain rudiments of any of the mouth-parts. The
under side of the head forms a deep hollow, and the mouth region is a
deep pit, bounded by a high, thin wall in front—the lower edge of the
clypeus. This pit is open to the roof of the mouth or clypeus. It is
impossible to distinguish the rudiments of any of the mouth parts, and
practically they appear to be wholly obsolete.

THE THORAX.

Notum.

This region of the body is more highly concentrated than in any other Phyloptera, not excepting the Trichoptera. The prothorax is a rather wide collar, longer and broader than in the Trichoptera, but the mesothorax is spherical and very large in proportion to the metathorax, which is rudimentary and but slightly developed; owing therefore to the large mesothorax and the small pro- and metathorax, the entire thorax is oval-elliptical, and much consolidated, thus approaching in its general appearance the general shape of the Tipulid thorax, or that of the lower Lepidoptera.

Pronotum. This forms a broad collar extending backwards on each side, the hinder edge being excavated in the middle.

Mesonotum. This is long and well developed, not so wide as the body, the flanks extending out, when seen from above, beyond the sides of the notum. The præscutum is well developed, forming a round, convex, swollen sclerite as long as broad, with a median suture-like impression. The scutum is very large and long, oval, about one-third longer than broad, slightly broader behind than in front.

The scutellum is large and well developed, irregularly scutellate in outline, with two bosses in front; the posterior end is narrow, truncate at the end, with the surface at the end somewhat swollen.

Metanotum. The metathoracic segment is small, very short, and the notum and sternum, as also the pleurites, are somewhat rudimentary. The surface of the notum is somewhat depressed below the level of the mesoscutellum. It is difficult to describe the sclerites, which are represented in Fig. 1. The entire segment is about one-third as long as broad. The scutum is not well differentiated, being represented by a median irregular area (Fig. 1 *se''*) about half as long as broad. No scutellum and postscutellum can be distinguished with certainty.

Pleurum.

The sclerites of the flanks are difficult to distinguish. In their development and arrangement the Ephemerina differ from all other Phyloptera.

Mesopleurum. Though there are a number of sclerites in the mesothorax it is difficult to distinguish what are properly episterna and epimera. The region of the mesepisternum is indicated in Fig. 2 *epis''*, and is much larger than the epimeral, which is the region situated over the insertion of the middle pair of legs.

The first pair of spiracles is situated on the mesothorax under and in front of the insertion of the first pair of wings; the second pair is situated on the metathorax directly under the insertion of the second pair of wings.

In the *metapleurum* the episternal region is quite limited and minute compared with the large mesepisternal region; what I am inclined to regard as the epimerum appears to be the sclerite *c m''* (Fig. 2), which in the sketch is situated directly under the metanotum.

Sternum.

Prosternum. This is a small triangular area situated between the insertion of the legs.

Mesosternum. This is a very large region divided into a præsternite and sternite. The former is narrow, as long as broad, the surface convex. The sternite is divided into two large, long, oval portions extending far back of the insertion of the legs.

Metasternum. This sclerite is very short, small and rudimentary.

THE ABDOMEN.

There are ten abdominal segments. The first tergite is wanting, the tenth is a supra-anal plate. There are nine urosternites; the basal is large and long, with a pair of spiracles. The 11th uromere may be represented by the median articulated appendage situated between the two very long multi-articulated cercopoda. The 10th urite is represented by two long, oval, parallel plates.

A remarkable feature of the male Ephemerina is the two pairs of jointed appendages rising from beneath the cercopoda. These may be regarded as homologues of two pairs of the rhabdites composing the ovipositor of the female of other insects. The lower pair (Fig. 1 *rh*) is 3-jointed (perhaps 4-jointed), while the upper pair (*rh'*) is 2-jointed. We know of no other insects which have two pairs of jointed claspers. These singular organs may be called *rhabdopoda*. They appear to be homologues of the abdominal feet of Myriapods, the abdominal legs of Tenthredinid and Lepidopterous larvæ, and the spinnerets of spiders.

The adult Ephemerina, then, in the lack of mouth-parts, in the concentrated thorax, and the possession of two pairs of abdominal jointed appendages, differ remarkably from the Odonata and other Phyloptera, so that we are nearly justified in regarding the group as entitled to rank as a suborder.

Order NEUROPTERA (as restricted by Erichson).

Suborder 1. PLANIPENNIA.

Family SIALIDÆ.

THE HEAD.

Corydalus cornutus. (Pl. LII, figs. 1–3.) Head very broad and flat; vertex remarkably large, broad, long, and flat, forming the bulk of the epicranium. Ocelli three, large, but the ocellar area is small, with no suture; the ante-antennal (orbital) fossæ large and conspicuous, transversely oval above, beneath curvilinear. No suture between the clypeus and epicranium, the very broad clypeus being indefinitely bounded behind, the front edge projecting over and concealing the short, broad labrum, and the edge thickened and tridentate. Mandibles of male enormous, their base partly covered by the clypeus. The genæ are very large and broad, bounded (in part) in front by the ante-antennal curvilinear fossæ. The gula is solid, long, and narrow, extending from the occipital suture to the mentum, there being no submental suture; lateral sutures separate the mentum plainly from the gulæ; submentum very broad. The occiput is present, appearing as a short and broad area, with a median, transversely-oblong sternite forming the base of the gula. (See larva.)

Raphidia oblita.[154] (Pl. LI, fig. 5–7.) Head as in Corydalus, but the vertex is longer in proportion and the clypeus, being smooth, is better limited. The ocelli are either present or absent, and there is no distinct area. The labrum is large, the clypeus not concealing it. There are no fossæ. The genæ are very large, meeting over the gula, which is obsolete, except in front, where it is broad and triangular, and forms a submental region. The occiput is apparently well marked, forming the neck, and with a suture in front.

THE THORAX.

Notum.

Pronotum of Corydalus, enlarged.

Pronotum (Corydalus). Large and square, about as long as broad; full in front and sinuous behind; somewhat hollowed in the middle.

Raphidia. (Pl. LIV, fig. 10.) Long and narrow, rectangular, very slightly excavated in front, and pointed behind.

Mesonotum (Corydalus. (Fig. 12). Præscutum broadly subtriangular, shorter than in Raphidia, but more distinct. Scutum completely cleft, the præscutum and sentellum touching; each division of the scutum subquadrate. Postscutellum large and long, very wide, and well developed.

Raphidia. (Pl. LIV, fig. 11.) Præscutum well developed, larger, but otherwise as in Corydalus. Scutum completely cleft, so that the præscutum meets the scutellum; the latter shorter than broad, obtuse at the apex in front, being subtriangular. Postscutellum well developed, wide, and of nearly the same length throughout, but incised in the middle to receive the scutellum.

Metanotum (Corydalus). Præscutum much as in Raphidia, but smaller; scutum not entirely divided; scutellum triangular, less acute in front than in Polystœchotes, but more so than in Raphidia. Postscutellum well developed, transversely linear.

---

[154] *Raphidia oblita* Hagen, from California.

Raphidia. (Pl. LIV, fig. 12.) Præscutum present, but obscurely marked, being almost obsolete, but the outline is seen to be triangular. The scutum is large, only half divided by the scutellum, which is much shorter than broad, but triangular in form. Postscutellum forms a narrow, transverse band, which is shorter than in the mesonotum.

Pleurum.

Corydalus. In the *propleurum* (Pl. LXIV, fig. 1) the episternum and epimerum are minute, rudimentary, and not well defined; owing to the great size of the sternite no trochantine is visible. The coxa is large and thick, about twice as large as the succeeding coxæ.

Raphidia. (Pl. LIV, fig. 13). Much as in Corydalus; the episternum and epimerum are minute and rudimentary, the relative form of these sclerites not being easily made out. The coxæ, however, are long and thick, and much larger than those of the meso- and metathorax.

In *Corydalus* (Fig. 2) the meso-flanks are rather short and thick; the supra-sternite square. The episternum is a little longer than broad; the suture between it and the sternito is obsolete. The epimerum is moderately long, widening considerably towards the insertion of the wings. The coxa is very short and thick. The trochantine is very small; one-half as large as the coxa.

Raphidia. (Pl. LIV, fig. 14.) The mesopleurites are just as in Corydalus, but longer and slenderer, and the suture of the sternum is well marked. The epimerum is longer and narrower above than in Corydalus, and the trochantine is small; coxa moderately large.

Metapleurum (Corydalus). (Fig. 12.) The flanks of the metathorax are longer, *i. e.*, thicker, than in the mesothorax; being also shorter vertically. The episternites are shorter vertically, but thicker, and the coxæ are shorter and thicker. The epimerum is undivided, not so wide above (next to the insertion of the wings) as in the mesothorax. The trochantino is a little smaller than in the mesothorax.

Raphidia. (Pl. LIV, fig. 15.) As in Corydalus, the metapleurites are decidedly thicker and longer than the pleurites of the mesothorax. The episterna are both larger and thicker than in the mesothorax. The epimerum is not divided, narrower below, and wider towards the insertion of the wing than in the mesothorax. The coxa is nearly twice as large as in the mesothorax.

Sternum.

Corydalus. The *prosternum* (Fig. 4) is remarkably large, square, with an anterior, short, separate piece, or præsternite.

The *mesosternum* (Fig. 5) is large and very broad, transversely sub-oblong, the suture between it and the infra-sternite only partial.

The *metasternum* is as in the mesothorax, but a little larger (Fig. 6).

Raphidia. The *prosternum* (Pl. LIV, fig. 16) is very large, long, and narrow oblong antero-posteriorly, and is covered by the bent-down

22 E O

tergite. The *mesosternum* (fig. 17) is large, each half subrhomboidal and passing laterally, forming a ridge between the sur- and infra-episternites. The *metasternum* (fig. 18) is much as in the mesosternum, there being no special difference in form or size, since the meso- and metathorax are of the same size.

THE ABDOMEN.

Corydalus. The ♂ abdomen (Pl. LVII, figs. 4–5; Pl. LVIII, fig. 1) is not very long, but broad and thick; ten uromeres; ten tergites, the tenth rudimentary and conical, concealed by the large ninth tergite, which is cleft, and bears two pairs of large, long claspers, which are jointed to the tergite. The pleurites are narrow, membranous. There are eight urosternites, the eighth cleft along the entire length.

Raphidia. The ♀ abdomen is moderately long, broad, spindle-shaped. There are ten uromeres; ten tergites, the tenth small. The pleurites are well developed, but narrow, bearing the spiracles. Of the urosternites, seven are well developed, and the ovipositor is remarkably well developed, more so than in any other Neuroptera (Pl. LVIII, fig. 5–7).

HEMEROBIIDÆ.

THE HEAD.

Ascalaphus.[155] (Pl. LI, figs. 3–4.) The head is held vertically; it is broad and short; the eyes are very large, approaching the Odonata in this respect, and are double. The epicranium is small and narrow on the vertex, owing to the large eyes, which nearly meet above. The orbits are very wide in front of the eyes; the clypeus broad, double, being divided into an anterior and posterior clypeus; the latter is smooth and flat, transversely oblong, limited on the sides by two deep linear fossæ; the anteclypeus narrows in front and is broadly trapezoidal, but is considerably shorter than the postclypeus. The labrum is broad and very short, the front edge a little excavated. The genæ are large, full, and swollen. The gular region is depressed, moderately wide.

Myrmeleon diversum Hag.[156] (Pl. LI, figs. 1, 2). The head is short and moderately broad; the vertex is full and swollen on each side of the median furrow. No ocelli, and no ocellar area, the latter region being sunken and obsolete. There are two deep, ante-antennal, linear, orbital fossæ in front at the base of the clypeus. There is no well-marked clypeal suture. The clypeus is a little shorter than broad, the posterior and anterior divisions being slightly indicated by a ridge. The labrum is short and broad. The gula is broad and membranous.

Polystœchotes nebulosus. (Pl. LI, figs. 8–10.) The head is of the same shape as in Myrmeleon, but the vertex is entire, full, and convex. Ocelli wanting, but the ocellar area is full, raised, though not well defined.

---

[155] *A. longicornis?* from New Jersey.
[156] The specimens examined were from Colorado. I am indebted to Dr. H. Hagen for the identification of the species.

The orbits are large. The orbital fossæ are round, but not so distinct as in Myrmeleon. The clypeus is as long as broad, the sutures more distinct than in Myrmeleon; the median transverse ridge is more distinct than in Myrmeleon. The post- and anteclypeus are nearly equal in size. Labrum as in Myrmeleon. The gula is broad, membranous.

Mantispa.[157] (Pl. LII, figs. 4-6.) The head is held vertically, and is as broad as long. The epicranium is broader than long, rather flat, with no V-shaped suture or ocellar area. The clypeus is large, very distinct, nearly as broad as long, square at the base, but constricted in the middle. The labrum is large, broader than long, much rounded and produced in front. The genæ are broad, and the gular region is rather narrow, but moderately so compared with Corydalus. The submentum(?) is large, and nearly as long as broad. The ligula is very large and long, spatulate, not divided, and very simple compared with Corydalus.

THE THORAX.

Notum.

In *Ascalaphus* the *pronotum* (Pl. LVI, fig. 1) is short and small, divided into two halves by a deep median suture. In its shape it approaches that of the Odonata more than any other true Neuroptera.

Myrmeleon. (Pl. LIV, fig. 1.) It is square, much excavated behind and full in front, a little narrower than long.

Polystœchotes. (Pl. LVII, fig. 8.) It is one-half as long as broad, and is a little excavated in front and behind.

Mantispa. It is very long, being twice as long as its greatest breadth, subpyriform in outline, nearly twice as broad in front (full on the front edge) as behind. It is excavated behind (Pl. LV, fig. 1).

The *mesonotum. Ascalaphus.* (Pl. LVI, fig. 2.) The præscutum is large with the central portion subcordate, larger than in Myrmeleon. The scutum is almost entirely divided. Scutellum large and swollen, apex very obtuse; the postscutellum forms a transverse, flat ridge.

Myrmeleon (Pl. LIV, fig. 2.) Rectangular in outline. The præscutum is very large, as long as broad, and much as in Polystœchotes. The scutum is not deeply cleft, the median third being entire. The scutellum is small, subtriangular, broad, and with the apex obtuse, while the side sclerites are large, as in the metanotum. Postscutellum?

Polystœchotes. (Pl. LVI, fig. 9). The præscutum is very large, being nearly as large and wide as the scutum, and divided by a median furrow; each half full and rounded in front. The scutum is completely cleft, the præscutum and scutellum touching; each side of the scutum is squarish. The scutellum is broader than long, very acute, being produced in front, forming a long point. The postscutellum is rather large and very wide, being divided by a median suture.

Mantispa. (Pl. LV, fig. 2.) Præscutum minute, nearly obsolete, not

157 *Mantispa brunnea* Say, from Utah; identified by Dr. Hagen.

visible from above. The scutum is, however, much larger than in any other genera of Neuroptera (restricted), being only cleft on the posterior one-fifth. The scutellum is very short and broad; one-fourth as long as broad, with a linear, depressed, acute apex. The postscutellum is not visible from above, and is only seen by examining the posterior aspect of the segment in dissected specimens.

The *metanotum* (*Ascalaphus*). (Pl. LVI, fig. 3.) Much smaller than the mesonotum. The præscutum is unusually large, with a swollen cordate portion. The scutum is entirely divided, the two halves widely separated, the præscutum and scutellum meeting, the point of juncture being very wide.

Myrmeleon. (Pl. LIV, fig. 3.) The præscutum is large, excavated in front, though not so large as in Polystœchotes; it is wider than the scutellum. The scutum is entirely divided into halves, so that the præscutum and scutellum touch each other. The scutellum is very full and rounded behind, as long as broad, not being triangular; the side pieces are large, seen from above.

Polystœchotes. (Pl. LVI, fig. 10.) Præscutum? The scutum is completely divided by the scutellum, which is acutely triangular. Postscutellum?

Mantispa. (Pl. LV, fig. 3.) The præscutum obsolete, not visible from above. The scutum is larger than usual, but only cleft on the posterior fourth of its length; the scutellum is short, acutely triangular in front, but very broad, and the sides in front are sinuous; it is smaller and narrower than in the mesonotum. The postscutellum is not visible unless the specimen is dissected, when it is seen to form the back of the segment.

Pleurum.

Propleurum (*Ascalaphus*). The pleurum is hard to describe from a single specimen, but the sclerites are much rounded, full, and swollen; the mesothorax is nearly one-third longer and thicker than the metathorax, while the thorax as a whole is spherical and much consolidated.

Myrmeleon. (Pl. LIV, fig. 7.) The episternum is nearly twice as large as the epimerum. The coxæ are very large and long.

Polystœchotes. The episternum is not so much larger than the epimerum as in Myrmeleon, but the coxæ are longer and slenderer.

Mantispa. The pleurites are very small; the episternum is very small, irregularly oblong; the epimerum is subdivided, small, narrow, but a little more regular and larger than the episternum. Coxæ very large and long; the trochantine submembranous.

Mesopleurum (*Ascalaphus?*).

Myrmeleon. (Pl. LIV, fig. 8.) The flanks are very broad and short, as a whole. The suprasternite present, very short and broad, equilaterally triangular in outline. The episternum is remarkably short and broad, triangular, being two-thirds shorter than in Polystœchotes. The

coxa is large, much broader than long, subrhomboidal. The mesostigmata or their peritremes are situated each on the front and upper angle
of the supra-sternite directly in front of the fore wings.

Polystœchotes. (Pl. LVI, figs. 8–15). The pleurites are not so broad
and short as in Myrmeleon. The supra-sternite is considerably longer
than broad, the apex toward the wings being conical. The episternum
is vertically oblong, quite regular, being considerably longer than broad.
The epimerum is moderately broad, square below. The coxa is moderately long, longer than broad; the trochantine regularly conical.

Mantispa. (Pl. LV, fig. 8.) The flanks of the meso- and metathorax
are of the same size and general appearance. The episternum and epimerum are each subdivided more or less regularly into two sclerites.
The epimerum as a whole is not so wide as the episternum. The coxa
is large, full, conical; the trochantine is minute, short, triangular.

Metapleurum (Ascalaphus?).

Myrmeleon. (Pl. LIV, fig. 9.) Although the meta- are not much
shorter than the mesopleurites, the episternum (which is subdivided into
an upper and lower sclerite) is smaller but nearly of the same shape as
in the mesopleurites, but the coxæ are larger and broader in proportion.
The supra-epimerite is very different, being as broad as long, not
widening above, and it is solid, with no membranous area; while the
infra-epimerite is a linear, antero-posterior ridge becoming triangular
behind. The coxa is considerably larger than in the mesothorax. The
trochantine is one-half smaller than that of the mesothorax.

Polystœchotes. (Pl. LVI, fig. 15.) The meta- are about one-third shorter
than the mesopleurites. The episternum is as in the mesothorax, but the
supra-sternite is fuller, more rounded next to the wings. The epimerum
is divided into a supra- and infra-epimerite. The coxæ are more rounded
and globose than in the mesothorax, while the trochantine is smaller and
not so wide in proportion.

There is a great difference between the thorax of Polystœchotes and
Myrmeleon, that of the latter being about twice as long as in the former;
in both, however, the metathorax is shorter than the mesothorax.

Mantispa. The metapleurites are a little stouter and thicker than the
mesopleurites, but have the same structure, though the coxæ are considerably shorter.

Sternum.

Ascalaphus?

Myrmeleon. (Pl. LIV, fig. 4.) The *prosternum* is rudimentary and
membranous.

The *mesosternum* (Pl. LIV, fig. 5) is large and well developed, sub-
cordate, deeply furrowed medially; about two-thirds as long as broad.
There is no suture between it and the infra-episternite.

The *metasternum* (Pl. LIV, fig. 6) is much smaller than the mesosternum, but from lack of alcoholic specimens I can not here describe it.

Polystœchotes. The *prosternum* is rudimentary and membranous.

The *mesosternum* is triangular, cordate, one-half as long as wide in front; distinctly separated by suture from the infra-episternite, with a deep median furrow. The meta- as the mesosternite, but one-third as long.

Mantispa. The *prosternum* is very long and narrow, and is well developed. The *mesosternum* is large, broad, about one-third as long as broad; not distinctly separated by suture from the episternum; in this respect the metasternum is the same.

THE ABDOMEN.

Ascalaphus. (Pl. LVII, figs. 6, 7.) The abdomen is moderately long, spindle-shaped, with nine uromeres.

Myrmeleon. (Pl. LVII, figs. 8–10.) Very long and slender, more as in Odonata than other Neuroptera, being slender, cylindrical. There are seven well developed tergites; the 8th and 9th small, the 9th being as long as broad. The pleurites are broad, well developed, membranous; the spiracles distinct. Of the urosternites the first is obsolete, followed by six well-developed ones; the 7th well developed, oblong. The ♂ claspers are well developed, and are much as in Odonata.

Polystœchotes. (Pl. LVIII, figs. 2–4.) The abdomen is much shorter and thicker than in Myrmeleon. There are ten tergites; the 2nd subdivided into two subtergites, appearing as if two tergites; the 8th is one-third as long as the 7th; the 9th one-half as long as the 8th; the 10th is broader than long, the end being subconical. The pleurites are broad, membranous, six pairs of spiracles visible. There are seven urosternites, the first membranous and obsolete; the seventh longer than the sixth. No uropods; the cercopoda rudimentary.

Mantispa.—Broad and large, nine uromeres; the first tergite very short; ninth uromere very short, with very short uropoda?

Family PANORPIDÆ. Plate LX.

THE HEAD.

Panorpa.[153] (Pl. LX, figs. 1–3.) No true occiput. The epicranium is swollen on the vertex, which is as long as broad; there is a small ocellar area, and a small inter-antennal area. The front of the head is remarkably elongated, and is formed by the great development of the clypeus. The labrum? The genæ form an elongated tract, and the gula?

The submentum is a little longer than the mentum, while the lingua is short.

The antennæ are very long and many-jointed, as in moths, and the minute mandibles are situated at the end of the snout.

[153]On sending the specimen, after dissection, to Professor Hagen, he kindly informs me that it is "perhaps *P. debilis* Westw."

THE THORAX.

The *pronotum* (Pl. LX, fig. 4) is very small and short, with a deep transverse, impressed line; on the median line it is excavated in front and behind.

The *mesonotum* (Pl. LX, fig. 15) is without a præsentum; the scutum is large, about two-thirds as long as broad, and well-rounded in front. The scutellum is small, transversely narrow oblong. The post-scutellum is moderately long, interrupted by the median line.

The *metanotum* (Pl. LX, fig. 6) is much shorter than the mesonotum, but of the same general shape; the scutellum is also of the same general shape, but a little longer. The postscutellum is as in the mesonotum.

Pleurum.

The pleurites in this family are very long and narrow, the thorax being much compressed, its general shape approaching that of the Trichoptera and Lepidoptera.

The *propleurum* (Pl. LX, fig. 7) is rudimentary, the episterna and epimera being membranous.

. The *mesopleurum* (Pl. LX, fig. 9) has the episternum undivided, and is moderately full in front. The epimerum is entire, narrow, a little shorter than the episternum, and not so broad. The coxa is rather slender; the trochantine long and narrow.

The *metapleurum* (Pl. LX, fig. 8) is as the mesopleurum, but the episternum and epimerum are decidedly shorter, and slightly broader in proportion. The coxæ are a little larger and thicker, while the trochantine is about the same.

Sternum.

The *prosternum* is linear and rudimentary.

The *mesosternum* is short and broad, much as in Lepidoptera.

The *metasternum* is much smaller and less distinct than the mesosternum.

Finally, in the thorax as a whole, and in the form of the pleurites and sternites, we have a striking approximation to the Lepidoptera.

THE ABDOMEN.

There are ten uromeres; ten tergites, the first very short and transversely linear, the sixth to tenth narrow; there are seven urites, very narrow, as long as broad.

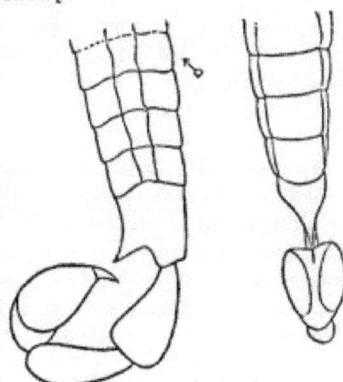

End of abdomen of male Panorpa, enlarged.

The pleurites are membranous, broad, having the spiracles, of which there are eight pairs as usual, the last pair minute.

Fig.   (in text) represents the end of the abdomen of the male of Panorpa.

Suborder 2. TRICHOPTERA. Plates LIX, figs. 1–5; LXI.

Limnephilus.[159] (Pl. LIX, figs. 1–5.) The head differs from all other *Phyloptera* in being constructed on a plan closely approaching that of the lepidoptera. It is short and high, and of the general proportions of the lepidopterous head. The vertex is as long as broad; the orbits wide. The clypeus is small, narrow, and situated high up; the labrum (Fig. 5) is small, narrow, elongate, subtriangular. (The exact differences from the Lepidopterous head are stated in the *American Naturalist,* Nov. 1871, vol. v, p. 711.) The mandibles are not present in Limne-philus, unless a slight pointed tubercle on each side of the lower part of the orbits (Fig. —, *md?*) may represent them. If so, they are consolidated with the epicranium, but I am inclined to think that these do not represent the mandibles at all, as rudimentary mandibles in the form of a movable tubercle are to be seen in Neuronia on each side of the base of the labrum.[160]

The maxillary palpi (Fig. 5) are long and slender, directed downward; the lobe on the side (Fig. 4, *lac.*) hangs down. It may perhaps be the homologue of the lacinia. The labial palpi are three-jointed (Fig. 5), while the mentum, palpiger, and an undivided rudimentary ligula are present.

The genæ are broad on the under side, while the gular region is narrow. The submentum is small and narrow; the mentum is trapezoidal, broadest in front.

THE THORAX.

Limnephilus. The *pronotum* (Pl. LXI, fig. 1) is much as in Lepidoptera, being divided into two transversely oval, narrow bosses by a deep median suture.

Mesonotum. (Fig. 2.) The patagia are thick, solid, rounded oval; longer than broad. The præscutum is obsolete.

The scutum is long and broad, with a prominent acute angle in the middle on each side. Surface with a deeply-impressed median line extending to the scutellum, and with a parallel, lateral impressed line. In general form there is a close approximation to the lepidopterous mesoscutum. It is deeply excavated behind for the reception of the scutellum, which is large, a little longer than broad, and subtriangular. The postscutellum is either wanting or it may be represented by a transverse ridge.

The *metanotum* (Fig. 3) is much as in the lepidopterous type. It is

---

[159] A common species, *L. pudicus* Hag.; identified by Dr. Hagen.

[160] In *Neuronia* they appear to be nearly of the same form as represented by Savigny in *Phryganea grandis* (Mémoires sur les Animaux sans Vertèbres. Pl. I, Fig. 1.) In the pupa the mandibles are much larger.

a little more than one-half as long as the mesonotum. The præscutum is well marked, small, divided by the median line into two transversely oblong pieces, the broad end next to the median line.

The scutum is deeply cleft behind for the reception of the triangular scutellum, the anterior part of the latter nearly reaching the front edge of the scutum. It is narrower than long, the lateral sutures obscure. The postscutellum is wanting.

Pleurum.

Propleurum. (Fig. 4.) The episternum and epimerum are minute, rudimentary.

Mesopleurum. The meso- and metapleurites are high and short; the metapleurites a little shorter than the meso-; in this respect much as in Lepidoptera. The episternum is not subdivided; it is square oblong, nearly three times as long (deep) as wide. The epimerum is narrower, but of nearly the same shape, but excavated by the wing-membrane. The coxæ are long, narrow, conical, as long as the episternite; the trochantine one-half as wide as the coxa.

Metapleurum. (Fig. 6.) The episternum is much narrower than the mesepisternum, especially towards the wings, and the epimerum is nearly as wide as in the mesopleurum. The coxæ are fuller and thicker than those of the mesothorax, while the trochantine is much smaller, being one-half as thick and shorter than in the mesothorax.

Sternum.

The *prosternum* is short, but distinctly developed. The *mesosternum* is rather large, about two-thirds as long as broad, produced backward in the middle, with a subacute apex. The *metasternum* is obsolete, represented by a membranous area.

THE ABDOMEN.

The abdomen (Fig. 7–9) is long and slender, cylindrical, much as in the lower Lepidoptera. There are nine uromeres equally well developed, the eighth not much smaller than the preceding one; there are eight urites, the eighth very short. The pleural region is membranous, broad, but obsolete on the first and eighth uromeres, with a spiracle in the middle of each of the first eight pleuritic areas.

It will be observed that the Trichoptera occupy a much higher systematic position than any of the foregoing groups. This is seen in the loss of two terminal segments in the abdomen, in the small concentrated head, and the subspherical thorax.

The Trichoptera and Panorpidæ differ from the other Neuroptera in having the trochantine well developed and nearly as large or larger than the coxæ; in this respect and in the form of the legs they closely resemble the Lepidoptera. Brauer* has called attention to the fact that in the Trichoptera and Panorpidæ the coxæ are divided into two halves.

23 E C

CHAPTER XII.

NOTE ON THE GEOGRAPHICAL DISTRIBUTION OF THE ROCKY MOUNTAIN LOCUST, ILLUSTRATED WITH A COLORED ZOÖ-GEOGRAPHICAL MAP OF NORTH AMERICA.

In the first report of the Commission (Chapter VI, p. 136) we traced the geographical limits of the Rocky Mountain locust, giving its eastern, northern, western, and its approximate southern limits; the latter being farther perfected and revised in Chapter VI of our second report, and in the colored map accompanying the report. On page 168 of our second report we also showed that the geographical limits of the western cricket (species of Anabrus) "are probably nearly or quite co-extensive with those of the Rocky Mountain locust."

For the convenience of the general reader, as well as of naturalists, we have, with the permission of Dr. F. V. Hayden, reproduced, with certain minor corrections, a colored zoö-geographical map of North America. It was originally prepared to illustrate the distribution of certain fresh-water Crustacea (Phyllopods) and appears in the Twelfth Annual Report of the United States Geological Survey of the Territories. Upon sending a proof to Mr. J. A. Allen, who has paid special attention to the geographical distribution of the mammals and birds, he kindly returned it without corrections, stating that it agreed with his views as to the limits of the zoölogical regions and provinces. Another copy was sent to Prof. A. E. Verrill, who made some corrections in the eastern province around the Bay of Fundy, and a few less important changes. Hence it is believed that the map will represent with tolerable accuracy the zoölogical distribution not only of the insects in general, but of nearly all the other classes of the animal kingdom, excluding the marine forms.

The range of the Rocky Mountain locust is co-equal with the light-brown area, *i. e.*, the Central Province, except that it will probably not be found south of the isothermal of 72°. This province is also the home of the species of Anabrus or Western Crickets. These are among the most characteristic Orthopterous insects to be found in this province, although there are many other species not to be found elsewhere. On the other hand, the common red-legged locust, *Caloptenus femur-rubrum*, occurs all over the Boreal or Canadian, the Eastern, the Western (Pacific), as well as the Central Province, so that it ranges over the whole of North America south of the limit of trees and north of Mexico and Lower California. The distribution of a third species, *Caloptenus atlanis*, is nearly co-extensive with that of *C. femur-rubrum*, although it

346

EXPLANATION OF PLATES.

LETTERING OF THE ANATOMICAL PLATES.

THE HEAD.
epic, epicranium.
cly, clypeus.
a. cly, anto-clypeus.
p. cly, post-clypeus.
lb, or lbr, labrum.
lb, labium.
gena, gena.
gula, gula.
ant, antenna.
e, eye.
oc, ocelli.
occ, occiput.
of, occipital foramen.
mx, 1st maxilla.
mx', 2d maxilla.
p, palpus.
c, cardo of maxilla.
st, sti, or stip, stipes of maxilla.
lac, lacinia of maxilla.
s. m., submentum.
m, mentum.
palpr, palpiger.
lig, ligula.
le, lamina exterior of ligula.
li, lamina interior of ligula.
md, mandible.

THE THORAX.
PRO, prothorax.
MESO, mesothorax.
META, metathorax.
n, notum of prothorax.
n', notum of mesothorax.
n'', notum of metathorax.
p. sc, prescutum of prothorax.
sc, scutum of prothorax.
scl, scutellum of prothorax.
p. scl, post-scutellum of prothorax.

p. sc' ⎫
sc' ⎪
⎬ the same sclerites of mesonotum.
scl' ⎪
p. scl' ⎭

THE THORAX—Continued.
p. sc'' ⎫
sc'' ⎪
⎬ the same sclerites of metanotum.
scl'' ⎪
p. scl'' ⎭
st, sternum of prothorax.
st', sternum of mesothorax.
st'', sternum of metathorax.
epis, episternum of prothorax.
epis', episternum of mesothorax.
epis'', episternum of metathorax.
em, epimerum of prothorax.
em', epimerum of mesothorax.
em'', epimerum of metathorax.
te, trochantine of prothorax.
te', trochantine of mesothorax.
te'', trochantine of metathorax.
cx, coxa of prothorax.
cx', coxa of mesothorax.
cx'', coxa of metathorax.
tr, trochanter of prothorax.
tr', trochanter of mesothorax.
tr'', trochanter of metathorax.
s.-epis, &c., sur-episternum.
s.-em, &c., sur-epimerum.
i.-epis, &c., infra-episternum.
i.-em, &c., infra-epimerum.
pes, leg.
pt, patagia.
W¹, front wing.
W², hind wing.

THE ABDOMEN.
A, abdomen.
c, cercopoda (cerci).
rh, rhabdite, or elements of the ovipositor, or clasper in the male.
ur, urosternite, or sternum of an uromere.*
tg, tergal sclerite or tergite.
pen, penis.
st, stigma or spiracle.
D, dorsal view.
L, lateral view.
V, ventral view.

* The author has sometimes inadvertently used the term urite instead of urosternite; Lacaze-Duthier's term urite is equivalent to our uromere.

The engraver has in some cases omitted the accents distinguishing the parts similarly lettered on the plates, but no confusion is likely to arise, upon careful examination of the figures and comparison with the text.

(1)

PLATE XXIII.

FIG. 1. *Forficula tæniata* Dohrn, head, upper side.

FIG. 2. *Forficula tæniata* Dohrn, head, under side; *lac*, lacinia; *le*, lamina exterior of ligula.

FIG. 3. *Forficula tæniata* Dohrn, head, side view.

FIG. 4. *Forficula tæniata* Dohrn, mandible.

FIG. 5. *Forficula tæniata* Dohrn, maxilla.

FIG. 6. *Forficula tæniata* Dohrn, 2d maxilla (labium); *l*, ligula; *le*, lamina exterior; *p*, palpus.

FIG. 7. *Forficula tæniata* Dohrn, pronotum, dorsal view.

FIG. 8. *Forficula tæniata* Dohrn, meso- and metanotum.

FIG. 9. *Forficula tæniata* Dohrn, pro-, meso-, and meta-thorax, sternal view.

FIGS. 10–12. *Forficula* larva, pro-, meso-, and metanotum; *not*, notum; *pst*, præ-sternum; *st*, sternum.

All enlarged. Drawn by C. F. Gissler, under author's direction.

PLATE XXIV.

FIG. 1. *Forficula*, American species. Propleurum: *not*, notum.

FIG. 2. *Forficula*, American species. Mesopleurum: *not*, notum.

FIG. 3. *Forficula*, American species. Metapleurum: *not*, notum.

FIG. 4. *Forficula*, American species. Prosternum.

FIG. 5. *Forficula*, American species. Mesosternum.

FIG. 6. *Forficula*, American species. Metasternum.

FIG. 7. *Forficula*, American species. Abdomen, lateral view: *c*, cercopoda.

FIG. 8. *Forficula*, American species. Abdomen, dorsal view: *c*, cercopoda.

FIG. 9. *Forficula*, American species. Abdomen, ventral view: *c*, cercopoda.

All the figures enlarged. Gissler del., under the author's directions.

(Pls. XXV–XXXII drawn by J. S. Kingsley.)

PLATE XXV.

FIGS. 1–14. Heads (front view) of typical Orthoptera.

PLATE XXVI.

FIGS. 1–13. Heads (top view) of typical Orthoptera. | FIGS. 14–27. Heads (side view) of typical Orthoptera.

PLATE XXVII.

FIGS. 1–14. Labium of typical Orthoptera.

PLATE XXVIII.

FIGS. 1–12. Maxilla (left) of typical Orthoptera. | FIGS. 13–20. Prothorax (tergal view) of typical Orthoptera.

PLATE XXIX.

FIGS. 1–13. Prothorax (lateral view) of typical Orthoptera. | FIGS. 14–16. Prothorax (tergal view) of typical Orthoptera.

PLATE XXX.

FIGS. 1–13. Meso- and metathorax (tergal view) of typical Orthoptera.

PLATE XXXI.

FIGS. 1–12. Meso- and metapleura of typical Orthoptera. | FIGS. 13–21. Prosternum of typical Orthoptera.

PLATE XXXII.

FIGS. 1–13. Meso- and metasternum of typical Orthoptera.

PLATE XXXIII.

FIG. 1–3. *Mantis carolina*. Prothorax.

FIGS. 4, 5. *Mantis carolina*. Meso- and metanotum.

FIG. 6. *Prisopus* (Brazil). Propleurum.

FIG. 7. *Prisopus* (Brazil). Meso- and metapleurum.

FIG. 8. *Prisopus* (Brazil). Prosternum.

FIG. 9. *Prisopus* (Brazil). Meso- and metasternum.

Gissler del

EXPLANATION OF PLATES.

PLATE XXXIV.

Figs. 1-8, 10, 11. Abdomen (tergal view) of typical female Orthoptera. Fig. 9. Abdomen (tergal view) of male *Diaphero-mera.*

PLATE XXXV.

Figs. 1-9. Abdomen (end, tergal view) of typical female Orthoptera. Figs. 10-16. Abdomen (end, tergal view) of typical male Orthoptera.

PLATE XXXVI.

FIGS. 1-9. Abdomen, side view, of typical female Orthoptera.

PLATE XXXVII.

NOTE.—Plates XXXVII and XXXVIII have been combined so that the explanations apply to Plate XXXVII, and there is no Plate XXXVIII.

PLATE XXXIX.

FIG. 1. *Termopsis angusticollis,* head, from beneath: *x,* hypopharyngeal chitinous support. (Gissler).

FIG. 2. *Termopsis angusticollis,* head, from above.

FIG. 3. *Termopsis angusticollis,* head, from side; the clypeus is shaded.

FIG. 4. *Termes flavipes,* head, from above: *s,* epicranial v-shaped suture.

FIG. 5. *Termes flavipes,* head, from side.

FIG. 6. *Psocus* sp., head, from above: *v,* v-shaped suture.

FIG. 7. *Psocus* sp., head, from side.

FIG. 8. *Pteronarcys californica,* head, drawn from the side.

FIGS. 1-5 drawn by C. F. Gissler; 6, 7, 8, by William W. Griffin: all magnified.

PLATE XL.

FIG. 1. *Pteronarcys californica,* head, upper view.

FIG. 2. *Pteronarcys californica,* head, under view.

FIG. 3. *Termopsis angusticollis,* 1st maxilla: *c,* cardo.

FIG. 4. *Termes flavipes,* 1st maxilla.

FIG. 5. *Pteronarcys californica,* 1st maxilla.

FIG. 6. *Pteronarcys californica,* 2d maxilla (labium).

FIG. 7. *Pteronarcys californica,* mandible.

FIG. 8. *Termopsis angusticollis,* labrum and part of clypeus.

FIG. 9. *Termes flavipes,* labrum.

Figs. 1, 2, 5-7 drawn by William W. Griffin; 3, 4, 8, 9, by Gissler: all magnified.

PLATE XLI.

FIG. 1. *Termes flavipes,* head seen from beneath: *mx,* maxilla; *palpr,* palpiger; *li,* lamina interior; *le,* lamina exterior; *p,* labial palpus.

FIG. 2. *Termes flavipes,* 2d maxilla (labium), seen from beneath.

FIG. 3. *Termopsis angusticollis,* 2d maxilla (labium).

FIG. 4. *Termes flavipes,* mandible, external view.

FIG. 5. *Termes flavipes,* mandible, internal view.

FIG. 6. *Termopsis angusticollis,* mandible, from within.

FIG. 7. *Termopsis angusticollis,* mandible, from without.

FIG. 8. *Termopsis angusticollis,* mandible, from without.

FIG. 9. *Termopsis angusticollis,* mandible, from within.

FIG. 10. *Termopsis angusticollis,* part seen beneath the labial palpi.

All enlarged. Gissler del.

PLATE XLII.

FIG. 1. *Termes flavipes.* Pronotum.

FIG. 2. *Termes flavipes.* Mesonotum.

FIG. 3. *Termes flavipes.* Metanotum.

FIG. 4. *Termes flavipes.* Propleurum.

FIG. 5. *Termes flavipes.* Mesopleurum.

FIG. 6. *Termes flavipes.* Metapleurum.

FIG. 7. *Termes flavipes.* Prothorax, sternal view.

FIG. 8. *Termes flavipes.* Mesothorax, sternal view.

FIG. 9. *Termes flavipes.* Metathorax, sterna view.

FIG. 10. *Termes flavipes.* Abdomen, tergal view: 1-10, the ten tergites; *c,* cercopoda.

FIG. 11. *Termes flavipes.* Abdomen, ventral view.

FIG. 12. *Termes flavipes.* Abdomen, lateral view, showing the 10 tergites and 9 urites.

All magnified. Gissler del., under author's direction.

(3)

EXPLANATION OF PLATES.

PLATE XXXIV.

FIGS. 1-8, 10, 11. Abdomen (tergal view) of typical female Orthoptera.

FIG. 9. Abdomen (tergal view) of male *Diapheromera*.

PLATE XXXV.

FIGS. 1-9. Abdomen (end, tergal view) of typical female Orthoptera.

FIGS. 10-16. Abdomen (end, tergal view) of typical male Orthoptera.

PLATE XXXVI.

FIGS. 1-9. Abdomen, side view, of typical female Orthoptera.

PLATE XXXVII.

FIGS. 1-6. End of abdomen, side view, of typical Orthoptera.

PLATE XXXVIII.

FIGS. 7-16. End of abdomen, side view, of typical female Orthoptera.

(Plates XXXIV-XXXVIII drawn by J. S. Kingsley.)

PLATE XXXIX.

FIG. 1. *Termopsis angusticollis*, head, from beneath: *x*, hypopharyngeal chitinous support. (Gissler.)

FIG. 2. *Termopsis angusticollis*, head, from above.

FIG. 3. *Termopsis angusticollis*, head, from side; the clypeus is shaded.

FIG. 4. *Termes flavipes*, head, from above: *v*, epicranial v-shaped suture.

FIG. 5. *Termes flavipes*, head, from side.

FIG. 6. *Psocus* sp., head, from above: *o*, v-shaped suture.

FIG. 7. *Psocus* sp., head, from side.

FIG. 8. *Pteronarcys californica*, head, drawn from the side.

FIGS. 1-5 drawn by C. F. Gissler; 6, 7, 8, by William W. Griffin: all magnified.

PLATE XL.

FIG. 1. *Pteronarcys californica*, head, upper view.

FIG. 2. *Pteronarcys californica*, head, under view.

FIG. 3. *Termopsis angusticollis*, 1st maxilla: *c*, cardo.

FIG. 4. *Termes flavipes*, 1st maxilla.

FIG. 5. *Pteronarcys californica*, 1st maxilla.

FIG. 6. *Pteronarcys californica*, 2d maxilla (labium).

FIG. 7. *Pteronarcys californica*, mandible.

FIG. 8. *Termopsis angusticollis*, labrum and part of clypeus.

FIG. 9. *Termes flavipes*, labrum.

Figs. 1, 2, 5-7 drawn by William W. Griffin; 3, 4, 8, 9, by Gissler: all magnified.

PLATE XLI.

FIG. 1. *Termes flavipes*, head seen from beneath: *mx*, maxilla; *palpr*, palpiger; *li*, lamina interior; *le*, lamina exterior; *p*, labial palpus.

FIG. 2. *Termes flavipes*, 2d maxilla (labium), seen from beneath.

FIG. 3. *Termopsis angusticollis*, 2d maxilla (labium).

FIG. 4. *Termes flavipes*, mandible, external view.

FIG. 5. *Termes flavipes*, mandible, internal view.

FIG. 6. *Termopsis angusticollis*, mandible, from within.

FIG. 7. *Termopsis angusticollis*, mandible, from without.

FIG. 8. *Termopsis angusticollis*, mandible, from without.

FIG. 9. *Termopsis angusticollis*, mandible, from within.

FIG. 10. *Termopsis angusticollis*, part seen beneath the labial palpi.

All enlarged. Gissler del.

PLATE XLII.

FIG. 1. *Termes flavipes*. Pronotum.

FIG. 2. *Termes flavipes*. Mesonotum.

FIG. 3. *Termes flavipes*. Metanotum.

FIG. 4. *Termes flavipes*. Propleurum.

FIG. 5. *Termes flavipes*. Mesopleurum.

FIG. 6. *Termes flavipes*. Metapleurum.

FIG. 7. *Termes flavipes*. Prothorax, sternal view.

FIG. 8. *Termes flavipes*. Mesothorax, sternal view.

FIG. 9. *Termes flavipes*. Metathorax, sterna view.

FIG. 10. *Termes flavipes*. Abdomen, tergal view: 1-10, the ten tergites; *c*, cercopoda.

FIG. 11. *Termes flavipes*. Abdomen, ventral view.

FIG. 12. *Termes flavipes*. Abdomen, lateral view, showing the 10 tergites and 9 urites.

All magnified. Gissler del., under author's direction.

EXPLANATION OF PLATES.

PLATE XLIII.

Fig. 1. *Termopsis angusticollis*, pronotum.

Fig. 2. *Termopsis angusticollis*, mesonotum: w^1, 1st pair of wings.

Fig. 3. *Termopsis angusticollis*, metanotum: w^2, 2d pair of wings.

Fig. 4. *Termopsis angusticollis*, propleurum.

Fig. 5. *Termopsis angusticollis*, mesopleurum.

Fig. 6. *Termopsis angusticollis*, metapleurum.

Fig. 7. *Termopsis angusticollis*, prothorax, sternal view: *pst*, præsternum; *not*, notum.

Fig. 8. *Termopsis angusticollis*, mesothorax, sternal view.

Fig. 9. *Termopsis angusticollis*, metathorax, sternal view.

Fig. 10. *Psocus novæ-scotiæ*, meso- and metathorax (notum), dorsal view: w^1, w^2, wings.

Fig. 11. *Psocus novæ-scotiæ*, metanotum, seen more from behind.

Fig. 12. *Psocus novæ-scotiæ*, meso- and metapleura.

Fig. 13. *Psocus novæ-scotiæ*, mesothorax, seen from in front.

Fig. 14. *Psocus novæ-scotiæ*, mesoscutellum.

All enlarged. Gissler del., under author's direction.

PLATE XLIV.

Fig. 1. *Pteronarcys californica*, propleurum.

Fig. 2. *Pteronarcys californica*, mesopleurum.

Fig. 3. *Pteronarcys californica*, metapleura.

Fig. 4. *Pteronarcys californica*, prosternum.

Fig. 5. *Pteronarcys californica*, mesosternum.

Fig. 6. *Pteronarcys californica*, metasternum.

Fig. 7. *Pteronarcys californica*, abdomen, dorsal view.

Fig. 8. *Pteronarcys californica*, abdomen, ventral view: *rh*, rhabdites.

Fig. 9. *Pteronarcys californica*, abdomen, lateral view: *br*, branchiæ or gills; *sp*, spiracles.

William W. Griffin del., under author's direction. All magnified.

PLATE XLV.

Fig. 1. *Ephemera (Leptophlebia) cupida?* Head and thorax, dorsal view: *pro-n*, pronotum; w^1, w^2, 1st and 2d pair of wings: 1, first abdominal segment.

Fig. 2. *Ephemera (Leptophlebia) cupida?* Head seen from beneath: *lb*, labium; *lp*, labial palpi; *mx*, maxilla; *st*, prosternum.

Fig. 3. *Ephemera (Leptophlebia) cupida?* Head seen from above.

Fig. 4. *Ephemera (Leptophlebia) cupida?* Head and prothorax, seen laterally.

Fig. 5. *Ephemera (Leptophlebia) cupida?* Meso- and meta-sternum: *sp*, spiracle.

Fig. 6. *Ephemera* sp., larva, head seen from in front: *md*, mandibles.

Fig. 7. *Ephemera* sp., larva, head seen from the side, the occipital region not drawn.

Fig. 8. *Ephemera*, pupa, head seen from in front.

Fig. 9. *Ephemera*, imago, head seen from above.

Fig. 10. *Ephemera*, imago, head seen from above, different view, more in front.

Figs. 1–5 drawn by Dr. C. F. Gissler; 6–10, author del.

PLATE XLVI.

Fig. 1. *Ephemera (Leptophlebia) cupida?* Male, much enlarged to show the structure of the notum and abdomen: *c*, corcopoda; *rh*, outer 3-jointed claspers or rhabdites; rh^1, inner pair of 3-jointed rhabdites.

Fig. 2. *Ephemera (Leptophlebia) cupida?* Side view of thorax: the lettering as in other plates.

Fig. 3. *Ephemera (Leptophlebia) cupida?* Side view of propleurum, with side view of notum.

Fig. 4. *Ephemera (Leptophlebia) cupida?* Abdomen, ventral view, showing the 9 urosternites.

Fig. 5. *Ephemera (Leptophlebia) cupida?* Abdomen, lateral view.

All the figures enlarged. Gissler del.

PLATE XLVII.

Fig. 1. *Æschna heros*, head, front view: *cl. p*, post-cl. a, ante-clypeus.

Fig. 2. *Æschna heros*, head, lateral view.

Fig. 3. *Æschna heros*, head, under view.

Fig. 4. *Agrion verticale?*, head, vertical view.

Fig. 5. *Agrion verticale?*, head, under view.

Fig. 6. *Agrion verticale?*, head, lateral view.

Fig. 7. *Æschna heros*, labium: 1, 2, 1st and 2d joint of labial palpus; *le*, lamina exterior of ligula; *li*, lamina interior.

Fig. 8. *Æschna heros*, maxilla.

Fig. 9. *Æschna heros*, mandible.

Fig. 10. *Agrion verticale?*, pronotum.

Fig. 11. *Agrion verticale?*, dorsal portion of meso- and metathorax, showing the great development of the episterna ($epis$) and epimera (em).

Fig. 12. *Calopteryx maculata*, pronotum.

Fig. 13. *Calopteryx maculata*, same as in Fig. 11.

All the parts enlarged; drawn by William W. Griffin, under author's direction.

EXPLANATION OF PLATES.

PLATE XLVIII.

Fig. 1. *Æschna heros*, meso-and metapleurum, and two abdominal arthromeres.

Fig. 2. *Æschna heros*, pronotum.

Fig. 3. *Æschna heros*, mesonotum.

Fig. 4. *Æschna heros*, metanotum.

Fig. 5. *Calopteryx maculata*, meso-and metanotum.

Fig. 6. *Calopteryx maculata*, pleurum of entire thorax.

Fig. 7. *Agrion verticale?*, propleurum.

Fig. 8. *Agrion verticale?*, pleurum of entire thorax, lettering as in Fig. 6: 1, 2, uromeres.

Figs. 1, 5, and 6 drawn by C. F. Gissler; figs. 3, 4, and 7, by William W. Griffin, under author's direction. Objects all enlarged.

PLATE XLIX.

Fig. 1. *Æschna heros*, abdomen, dorsal view, showing the 11 tergites: c, cercopoda. (1–11).

Fig. 2. *Æschna heros*, abdomen, lateral view.

Fig. 3. *Æschna heros*, abdomen, ventral view, the 11th tergite (11) seen from beneath: t, testes; ur, urosternites.

William W. Griffin del.

PLATE L.

Fig. 1. *Æschna heros*, end of female abdomen, showing the ovipositor: ur, urosternite; or, outer; mr, middle; ir, inner rhabdites or elements of the ovipositor; 11, 11th tergite; c, cercopoda; 1 and 2, uromeres, showing the external genital armature, the tergites widely separated.

Fig. 2. *Æschna heros*, male: pen, penis; tg, tergite; cl, clasper (basirhabdite); ur, urosternite of 2d uromere.

Fig. 3. *Æschna heros*, the same, with the tergites closed.

Fig. 4. *Agrion verticale?*, abdomen of male, side view: pen, penis; c, cercopoda.

Fig. 5. *Agrion verticale?*, abdomen of male, ventral view: ur, urosternite.

Fig. 6. *Agrion verticale?*, abdomen of male, end: 11, 11th tergite.

William W. Griffin del. All the parts enlarged.

PLATE LI.

Fig. 1. *Myrmeleon diversum*, head from above.

Fig. 2. *Myrmeleon diversum*, head from beneath; of, occipital foramen.

Fig. 3. *Ascalaphus longicornis?*, head from above; and beneath: epic, epicranium.

Fig. 4. *Ascalaphus*, head from beneath.

Fig. 5. *Raphidia oblita*, head from above.

Fig. 6. *Raphidia oblita*, head from beneath.

Fig. 7. *Raphidia oblita*, head from side; oc, occiput.

Fig. 8. *Polystœchotes nebulosus*, head from above.

Fig. 9. *Polystœchotes nebulosus*, head from beneath.

Fig. 10. *Polystœchotes nebulosus*, head from side.

William W. Griffin del. All the figures drawn enlarged.

PLATE LII.

Fig. 1. *Corydalus cornutus*, head seen from beneath.

Fig. 2. *Corydalus cornutus*, head seen from above: a. cly, ante-clypeus; p. cly, post-clypeus.

Fig. 3. *Corydalus cornutus*, head seen sidewise.

Fig. 4. *Mantispa brunnea*, head seen sidewise.

Fig. 5. *Mantispa brunnea*, head seen from above.

Fig. 6. *Mantispa brunnea*, head seen from beneath.

All enlarged. Gissler del., under author's direction.

PLATE LIII.

Fig. 1. *Mantispa brunnea*, 1st maxilla: c, cardo; st, stipes; l, lacinia; g, gula; p, palpus.

Fig. 2. *Ascalaphus longicornis*, 1st maxilla.

Fig. 3. *Myrmeleon diversum*, 1st maxilla.

Fig. 4. *Corydalus cornutus*, 1st maxilla.

Fig. 5. *Mantispa brunnea*, 2d maxilla (labium).

Fig. 6. *Ascalaphus longicornis?*, 2d maxilla (labium).

Fig. 7. *Raphidia oblita*, 2d maxilla (labium).

Fig. 8. *Myrmeleon diversum*, 2d maxilla (labium).

Fig. 9. *Corydalus cornutus*, 2d maxilla (labium).

All enlarged. William W. Griffin del., under author's direction.

(5)

EXPLANATION OF PLATES.

PLATE LIV.

Fig. 1. *Myrmeleon diversum*, pronotum.
Fig. 2. *Myrmeleon diversum*, mesonotum.
Fig. 3. *Myrmeleon diversum*, metanotum.
Fig. 4. *Myrmeleon diversum*, prosternum.
Fig. 5. *Myrmeleon diversum*, mesosternum.
Fig. 6. *Myrmeleon diversum*, metasternum.
Fig. 7. *Myrmeleon diversum*, propleurum.
Fig. 8. *Myrmeleon diversum*, mesopleurum.
Fig. 9. *Myrmeleon diversum*, metapleurum.

Fig. 10. *Raphidia oblita*, pronotum.
Fig. 11. *Raphidia oblita*, mesonotum.
Fig. 12. *Raphidia oblita*, metanotum.
Fig. 13. *Raphidia oblita*, propleurum.
Fig. 14. *Raphidia oblita*, mesopleurum.
Fig. 15. *Raphidia oblita*, metapleurum.
Fig. 16. *Raphidia oblita*, prosternum.
Fig. 17. *Raphidia oblita*, mesosternum.
Fig. 18. *Raphidia oblita*, metasternum.

All magnified. William W. Griffin del., under author's direction.

PLATE LV.

Fig. 1. *Mantispa brunnea*, pronotum.
Fig. 2. *Mantispa brunnea*, mesonotum.
Fig. 3. *Mantispa brunnea*, metanotum.
Fig. 4. *Mantispa brunnea*, prosternum.
Fig. 5. *Mantispa brunnea*, mesosternum.

Fig. 6. *Mantispa brunnea*, metasternum.
Fig. 7. *Mantispa brunnea*, propleurum.
Fig. 8. *Mantispa brunnea*, mesopleurum.
Fig. 9. *Mantispa brunnea*, metapleurum.

All enlarged. William W. Griffin del.

PLATE LVI.

Fig. 1. *Ascalaphus longicornis?*, pronotum.
Fig. 2. *Ascalaphus longicornis?*, mesonotum.
Fig. 3. *Ascalaphus longicornis?*, metanotum.
Fig. 4. *Ascalaphus longicornis?*, mesopleurum.
Fig. 5. *Ascalaphus longicornis?*, metapleurum.
Fig. 6. *Ascalaphus longicornis?*, mesosternum.
Fig. 7. *Ascalaphus longicornis?*, metasternum.
Fig. 8. *Polystœchotes nebulosus*, pronotum.
Fig. 9. *Polystœchotes nebulosus*, mesonotum: w¹, 1st wings.

Fig. 10. *Polystœchotes nebulosus*, metanotum: w², 2d wings.
Fig. 11. *Polystœchotes nebulosus*, mesosternum.
Fig. 12. *Polystœchotes nebulosus*, metasternum.
Fig. 13. *Polystœchotes nebulosus*, pronotum, seen laterally.
Fig. 14. *Polystœchotes nebulosus*, mesopleurum.
Fig. 15. *Polystœchotes nebulosus*, metapleurum.

All enlarged. William W. Griffin del., under author's direction.

PLATE LVII.

Fig. 1. *Pteronarcys californica*, pronotum.
Fig. 2. *Pteronarcys californica*, mesonotum.
Fig. 3. *Pteronarcys californica*, metanotum.
Fig. 4. *Corydalus cornutus*, end of abdomen of male, under side.
Fig. 5. *Corydalus cornutus*, end of abdomen of male, side view: c, cercopoda; rh, rhabdite.

Fig. 6. *Ascalaphus longicornis?*, abdomen.
Fig. 7. *Ascalaphus longicornis?*, abdomen.
Fig. 8. *Myrmeleon diversum*, abdomen of male, dorsal view.
Fig. 9. *Myrmeleon diversum*, abdomen of male, lateral view.
Fig. 10. *Myrmeleon diversum*, abdomen of male, ventral view.

All enlarged. William Griffin del.

PLATE LVIII.

Fig. 1. *Corydalus cornutus*, abdomen, dorsal view: c, cercopoda.
Fig. 2. *Polystœchotes nebulosus*, abdomen, dorsal view: c, cercopoda.
Fig. 3. *Polystœchotes nebulosus*, abdomen, ventral view: c, cercopoda.

Fig. 4. *Polystœchotes nebulosus*, abdomen, lateral view: c, cercopoda.
Fig. 5. *Raphidia oblita*, abdomen, dorsal view.
Fig. 6. *Raphidia oblita*, abdomen, lateral view.
Fig. 7. *Raphidia oblita*, abdomen, ventral view.

All enlarged. William W. Griffin del., under author's direction.

PLATE LIX.

Fig. 1. *Limnephilus pudicus*, head, seen from above: p, labial palpus.
Fig. 2. *Limnephilus pudicus*, head, seen from beneath.
Fig. 3. *Limnephilus pudicus*, head, seen from the side.
Fig. 4. *Limnephilus pudicus*: mx, 1st maxilla, lre, lacinia?
Fig. 5. *Limnephilus pudicus*, labrum.

Fig. 6. *Panorpa debilis?*, mouth-parts, showing labrum beneath.
Fig. 7. *Panorpa debilis?*, 2d maxilla (labium): palpg, palpiger; p, labial palpus.
Fig. 8. *Panorpa debilis?*, labrum.
Fig. 9. *Panorpa debilis?*, mandible.
Fig. 10. *Panorpa debilis?*, maxilla and one palpus.

All magnified. Gissler del., under author's direction.

(6)

EXPLANATION OF PLATES.

PLATE LX.

Fig. 1. *Panorpa debilis?*, head, view from above.
Fig. 2. *Panorpa debilis?*, head, view from beneath.
Fig. 3. *Panorpa debilis?*, head, view from side.
Fig. 4. *Panorpa debilis?*, pronotum.
Fig. 5. *Panorpa debilis?*, mesonotum.
Fig. 6. *Panorpa debilis?*, metanotum.
Fig. 7. *Panorpa debilis?*, propleurum.

Fig. 8. *Panorpa debilis?*, mesopleurum.
Fig. 9. *Panorpa debilis?*, metapleurum.
Fig. 10. *Panorpa debilis?*, end of abdomen from the side; female, somewhat compressed.
Fig. 11. *Panorpa debilis?*, end of abdomen from above: *c*, jointed cercopoda.

All enlarged. Figs. 1–9 drawn by William W. Griffin; 10 and 11, by C. F. Gissler.

PLATE LXI.

Fig. 1. *Limnephilus pudicus*, pronotum.
Fig. 2. *Limnephilus pudicus*, mesonotum.
Fig. 3. *Limnephilus pudicus*, metanotum.
Fig. 4. *Limnephilus pudicus*, propleurum.
Fig. 5. *Limnephilus pudicus*, mesopleurum.
Fig. 6. *Limnephilus pudicus*, metapleurum.

Fig. 7. *Limnephilus pudicus*, abdomen.
Fig. 8. *Limnephilus pudicus*, abdomen, end; dorsal view.
Fig. 9. *Limnephilus pudicus*, abdomen, end; ventral view.

All enlarged. Gissler del., under author's direction.

PLATE LXIV.

Fig. 1. *Corydalus cornutus*, propleurum.
Fig. 2. *Corydalus cornutus*, mesopleurum.
Fig. 3. *Corydalus cornutus*, metapleurum.
Fig. 4. *Corydalus cornutus*, prosternum.

Fig. 5. *Corydalus cornutus*, mesosternum.
Fig. 6. *Corydalus cornutus*, metasternum.
Fig. 7. *Corydalus cornutus*, mesonotum.
Fig. 8. *Corydalus cornutus*, metanotum.

(7)

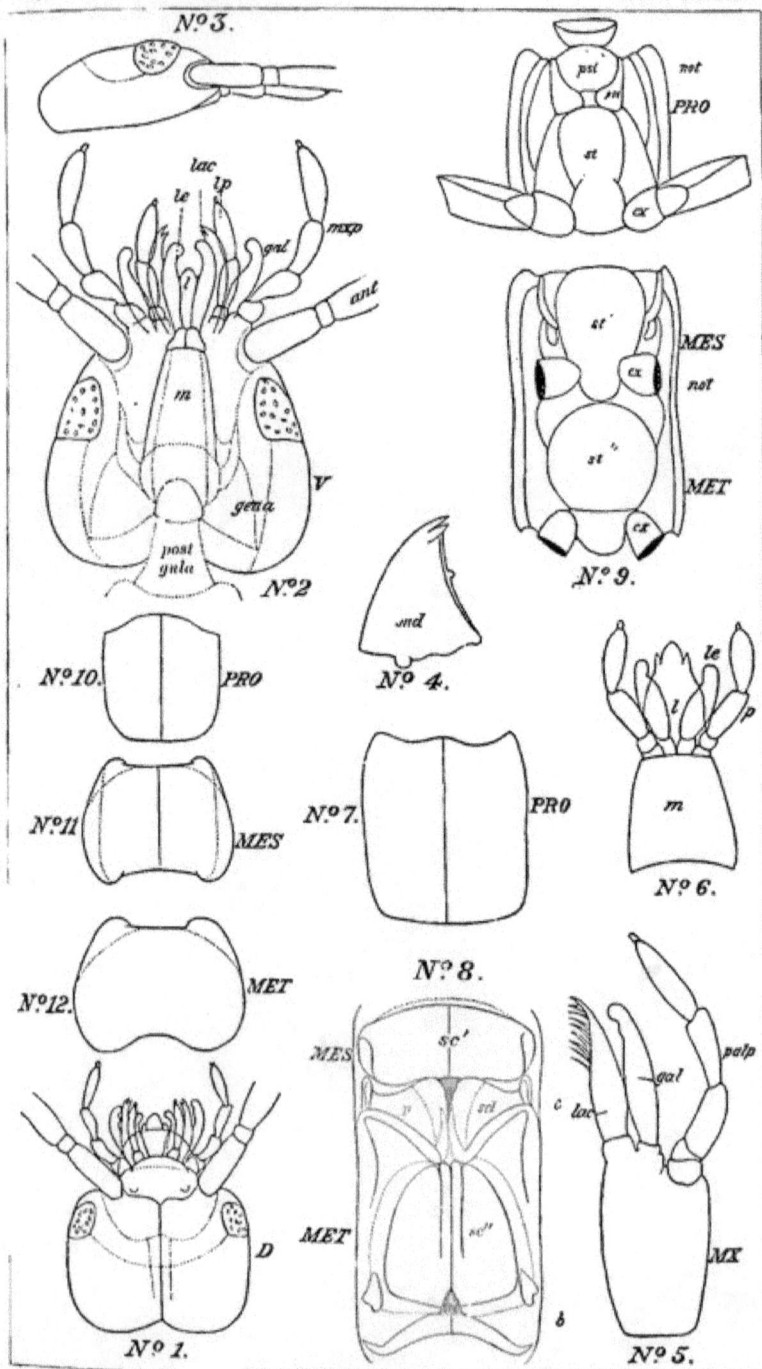

1-9. FORFICULA TÆNIATA.   10-12. FORFICULA, LARVA.

Plate XXIV.

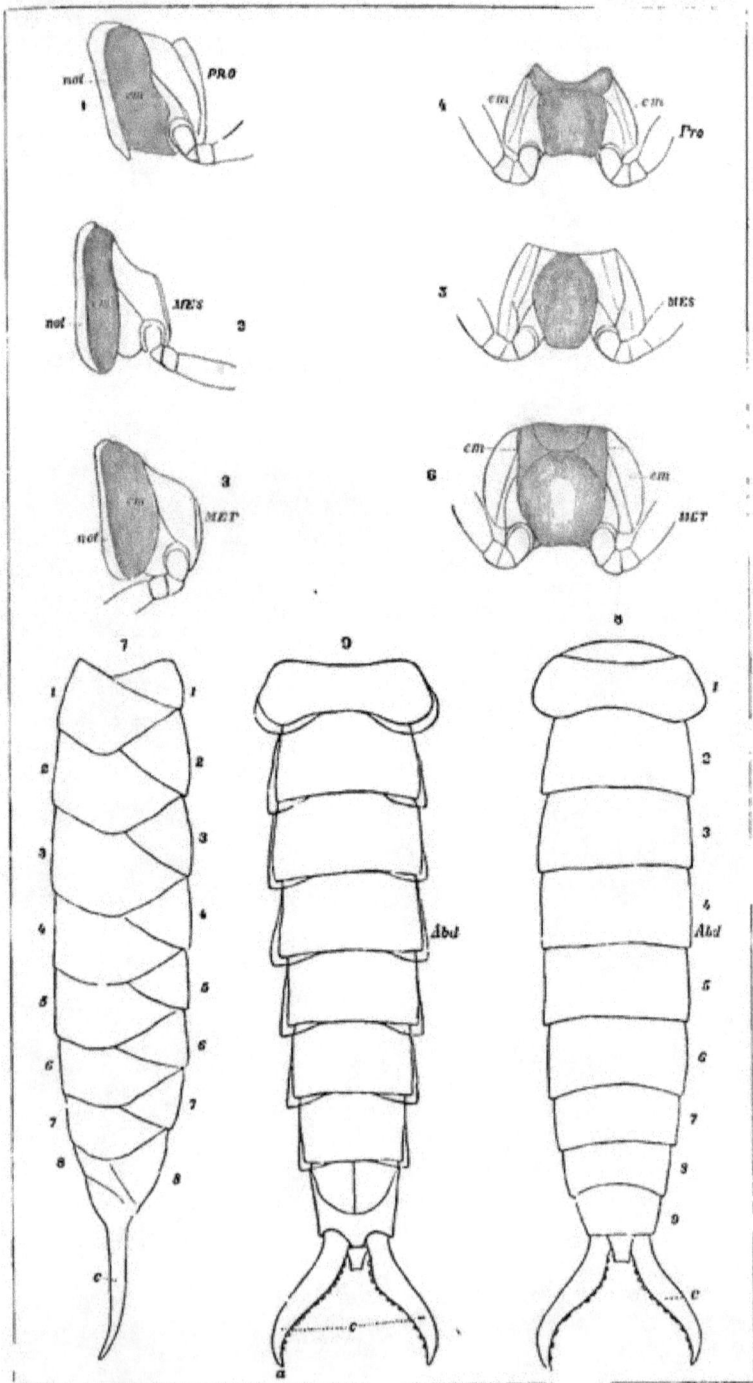

FORFICULA.

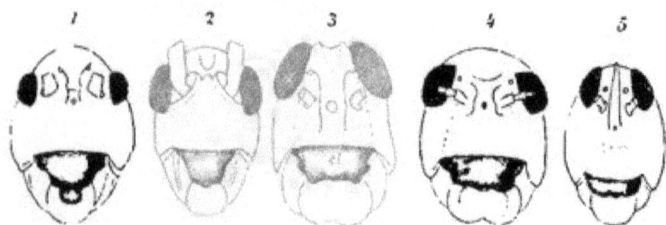

Anabrus.   Phaneroptera   Caloptenus   Tropidacris.   Tettix

Conocephalus.

Gryllus.

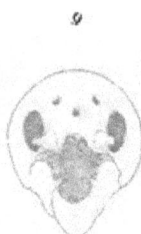

Gryllotalpa

Œcanthus

Truxalis

Diapheromera.

Periplaneta

Proscopia

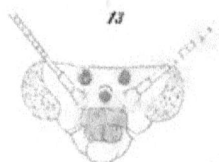

Mantis.

Œcanthus

Diapheromera

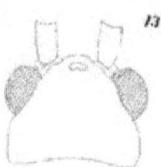

Prisopus

Truxalis

Proscopia

Conocephalus

Tropidacris

Tettix.

Caloptenus

Anabrus.

Gryllus

Gryllotalpa

Phaneroptera

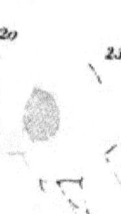

Œcanthus

Diapheromera

Periplaneta

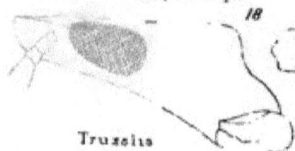

Truxalis

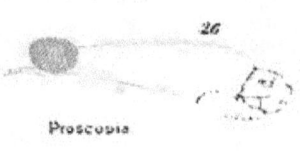

Proscopia

Prisopus

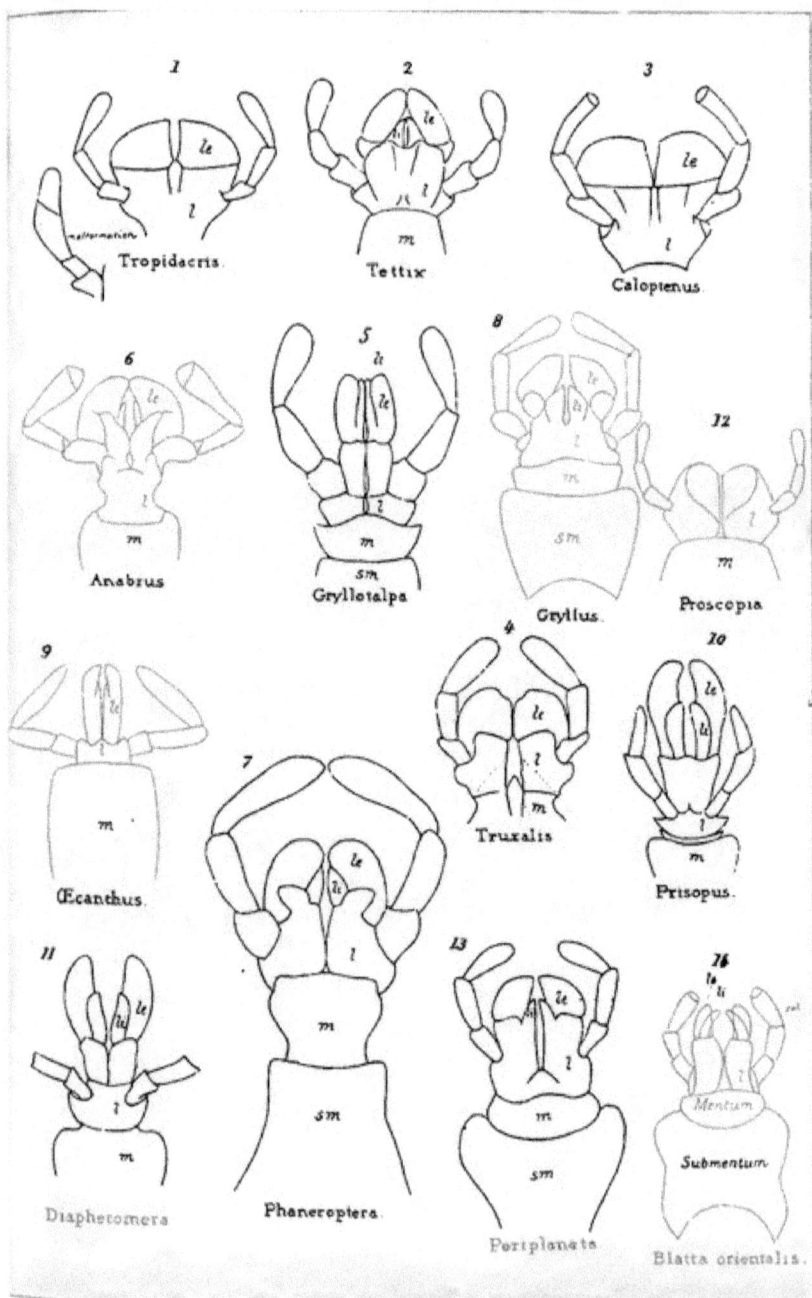

ORTHOPTERA; SECOND MAXILLA (LABIUM).

ORTHOPTERA; FIG 1-12 LEFT MAXILLA; 13-20, PRONOTUM.

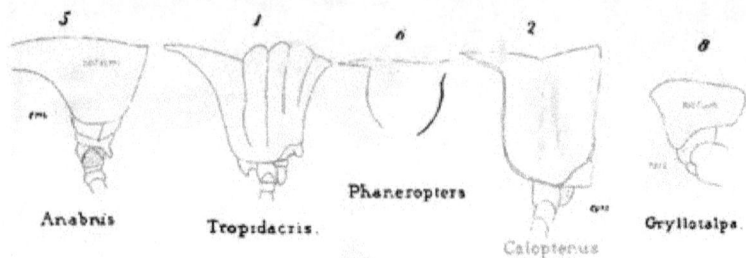

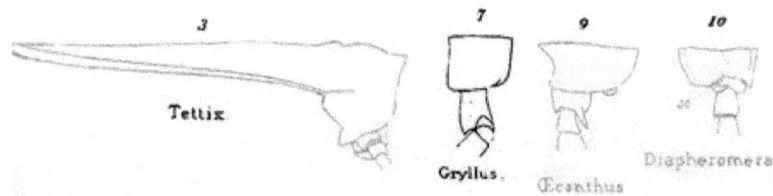

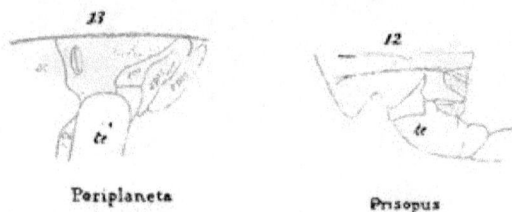

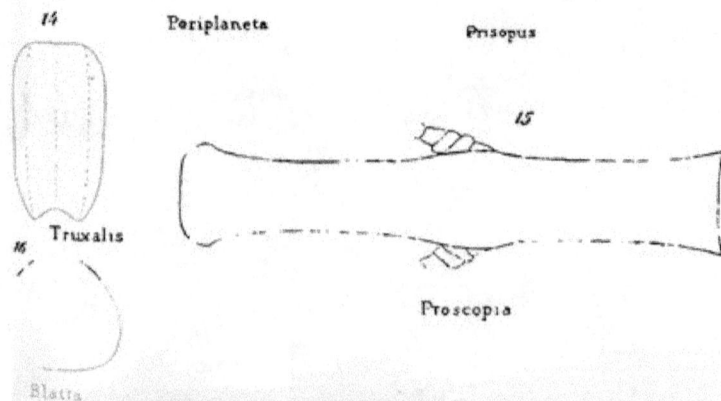

5 — Anabrus

1 — Tropidacris.

6 — Phaneroptera

2 — Calopterus

8 — Gryllotalpa.

3 — Tettix

7 — Gryllus.

9 — Œcanthus

10 — Diapheromera

13 — Periplaneta

12 — Prisopus

14 — Truxalis

16 — Blatta

15 — Proscopia

ORTHOPTERA. PROTHORAX LATERAL AND TOP VIEW

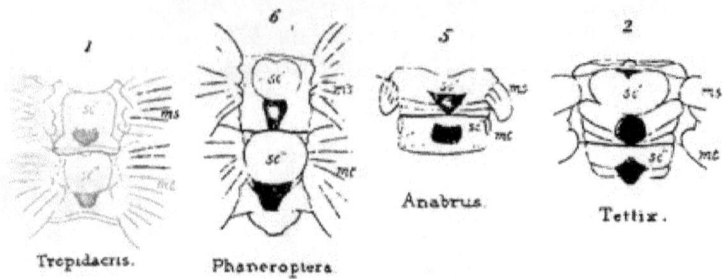

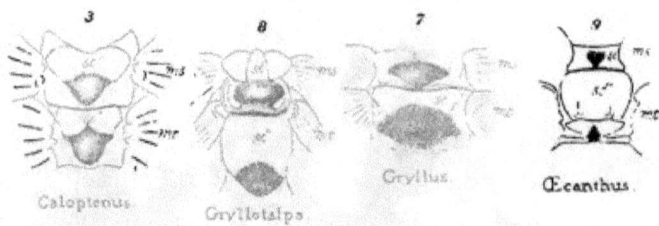

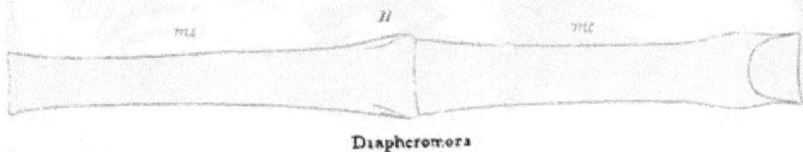

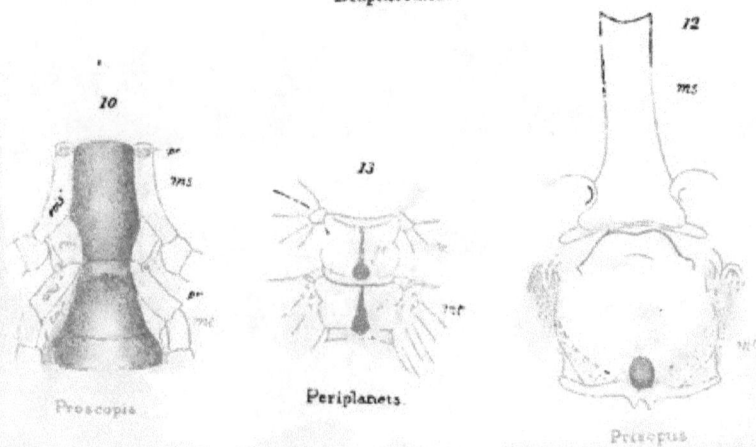

1 Tropidacris.

6 Phaneroptera.

5 Anabrus.

2 Tettix.

3 Caloptenus.

8 Gryllotalpa.

7 Gryllus.

9 Œcanthus.

11 Diapheromera.

10 Proscopia.

13 Periplaneta.

12 Proscopia.

ORTHOPTERA, MESO AND METANOTUM

PLATE XXXI

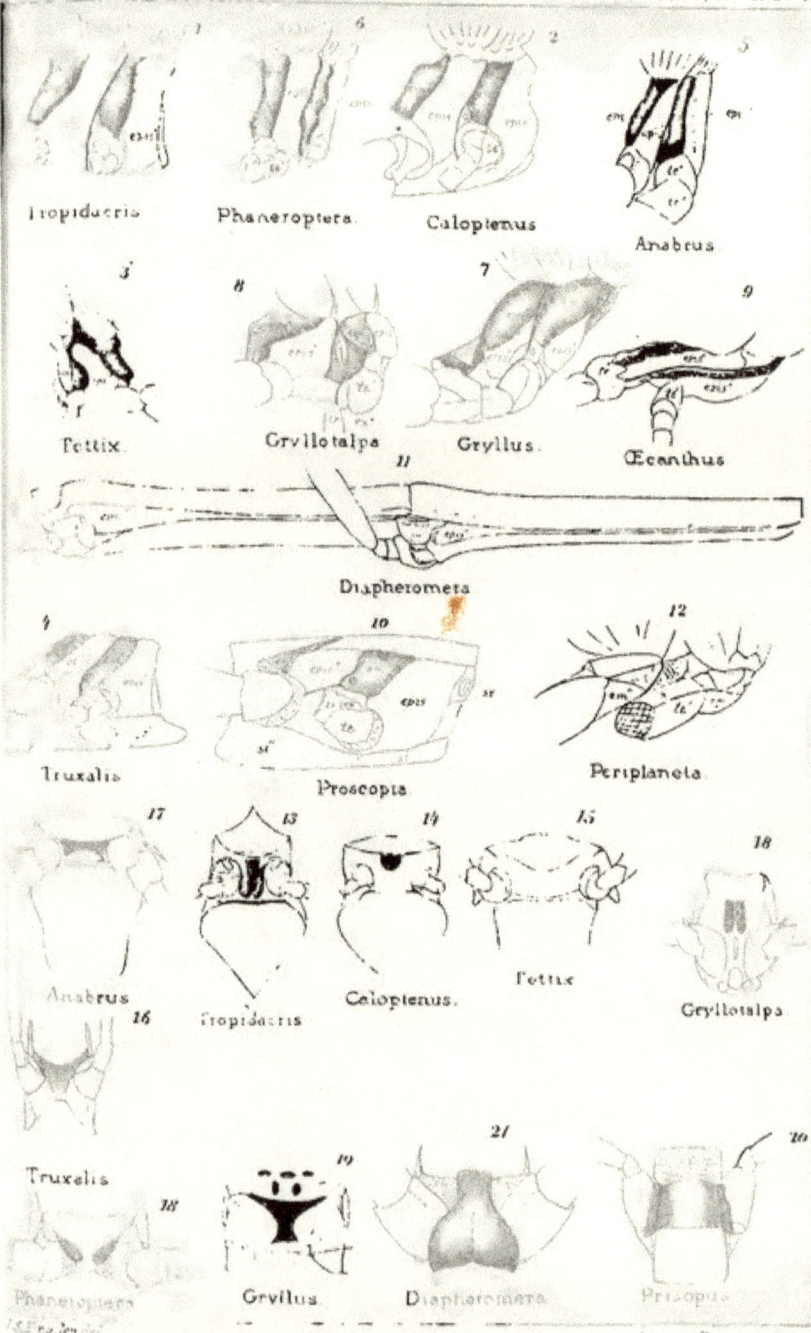

Tropidacris   Phaneroptera   Caloptenus   Anabrus

Tettix   Gryllotalpa   Gryllus   Œcanthus

Diapheromera

Truxalis   Proscopia   Periplaneta

Anabrus   Tropidacris   Caloptenus   Tettix   Gryllotalpa

Truxalis   Phaneroptera   Gryllus   Diapheromera   Proscopia

ORTHOPTERA 1 12 PLEURITES 13 21 STERNUM

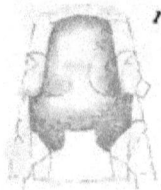

1

Tryxalis

6

Phaneroptera

5

Anabrus

3

Tettix

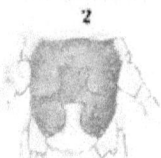

2

Caloptenus.

8

Gryllotalpa

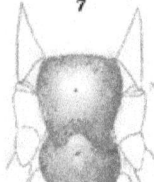

7

Gryllus

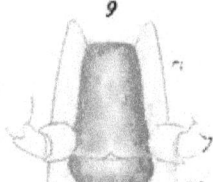

9

Œcanthus

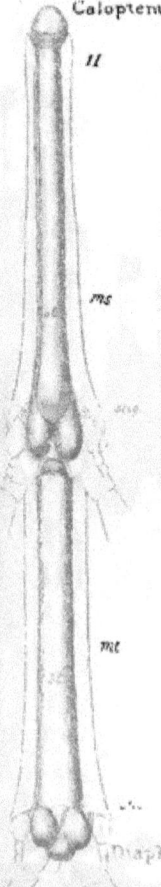

11

Diapheromera

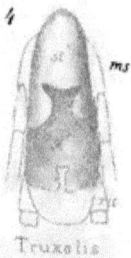

4

Truxalis

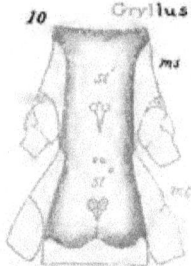

10

Proscopia

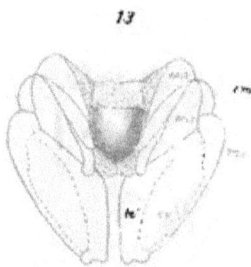

12

Mantis

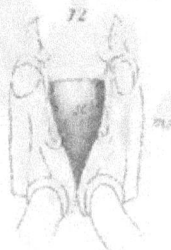

13

Periplaneta

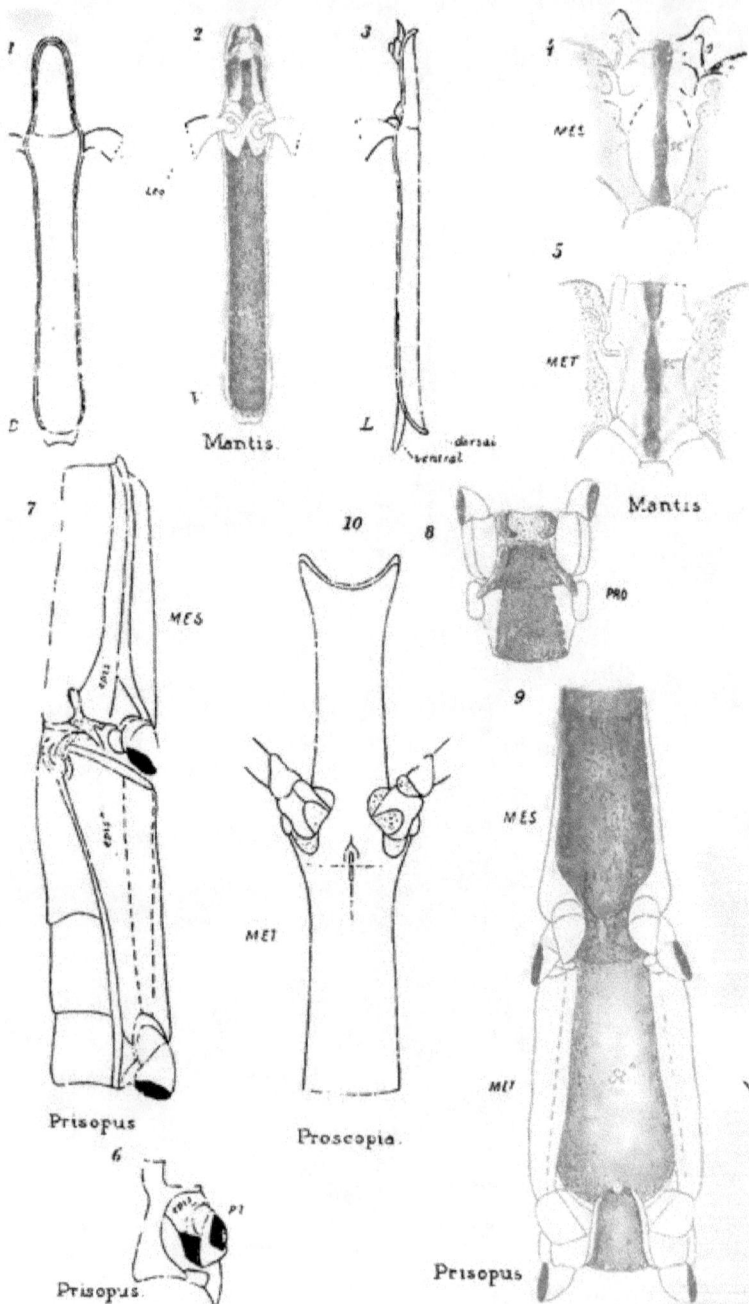

1

2

Mantis.

3

L   dorsal
ventral

4

MES   *SC*

5

MET

Mantis

7

MES

Prisopus

10

8

PRO

Proscopia.

9

MES

MET

Prisopus

6

P1

Prisopus.

Prisopus

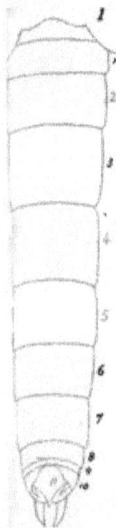
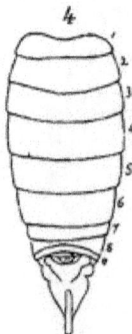
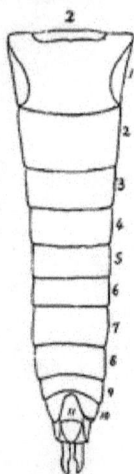
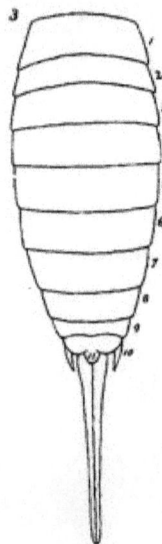
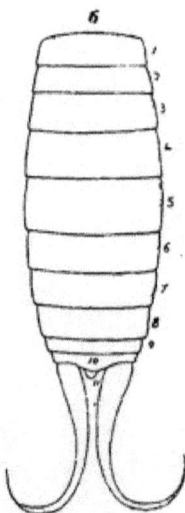

Phaneroptera.

Caloptenus.

Tropidactus.

Anabrus.

Gryllotalpa.

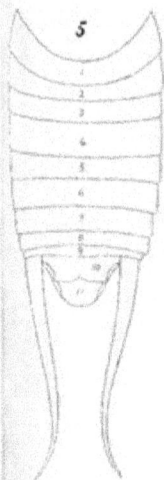
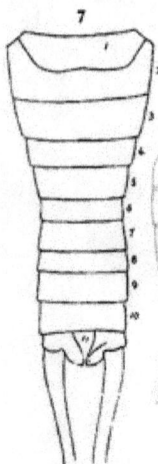

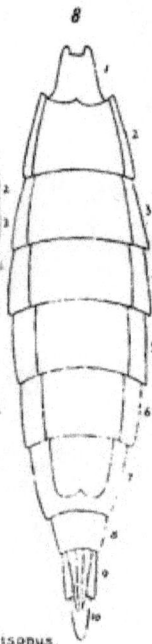

Periplaneta

Gryllus.

Œcanthus.

Prisopus.

Proscopia

Diapheromera.

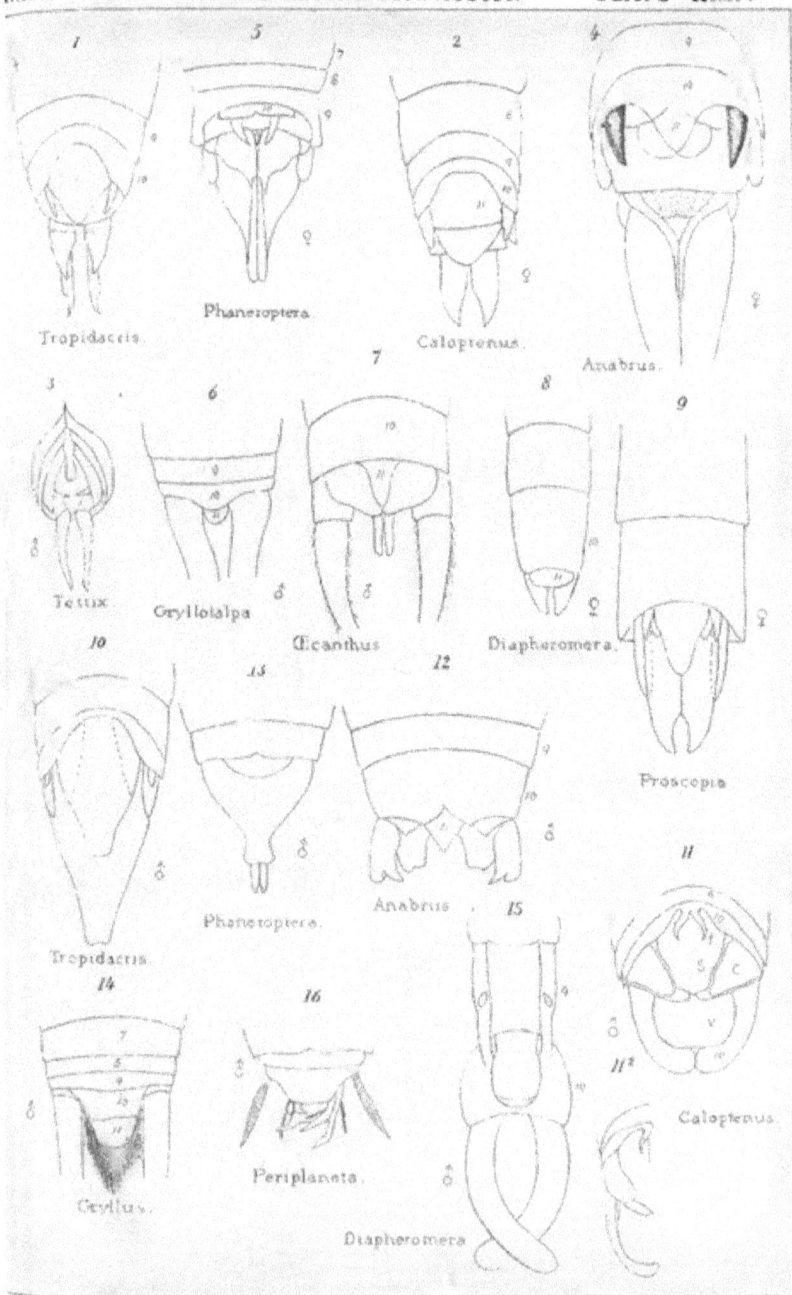

ORTHOPTERA, END OF ABDOMEN.

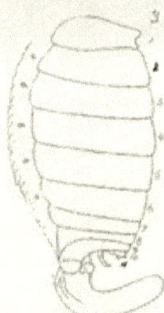

Phaneroptera.

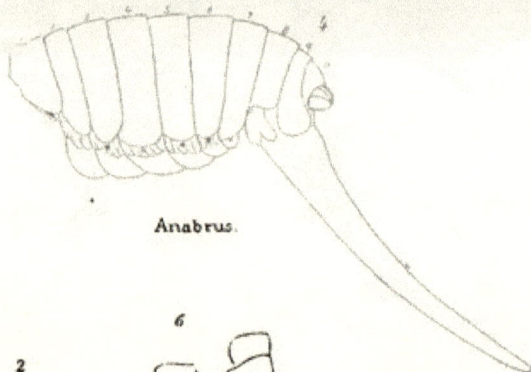

Anabrus.

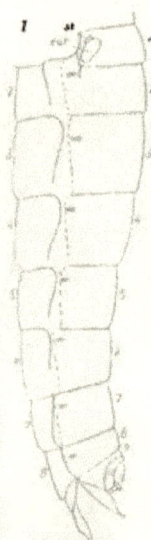

Tropidacris

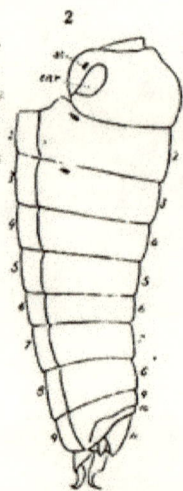

Caloptenus.

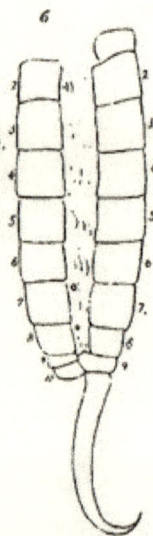

Gryllus.

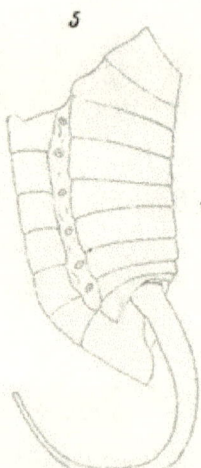

Gryllotalpa

Periplaneta.

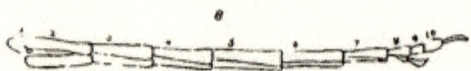

Diapheromera

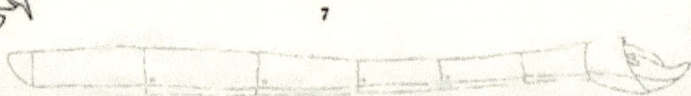

Proscopia

ORTHOPTERA, ABDOMEN, LATERAL VIEW.

Heliotype Printing Co   Boston

J S Kingsley del.

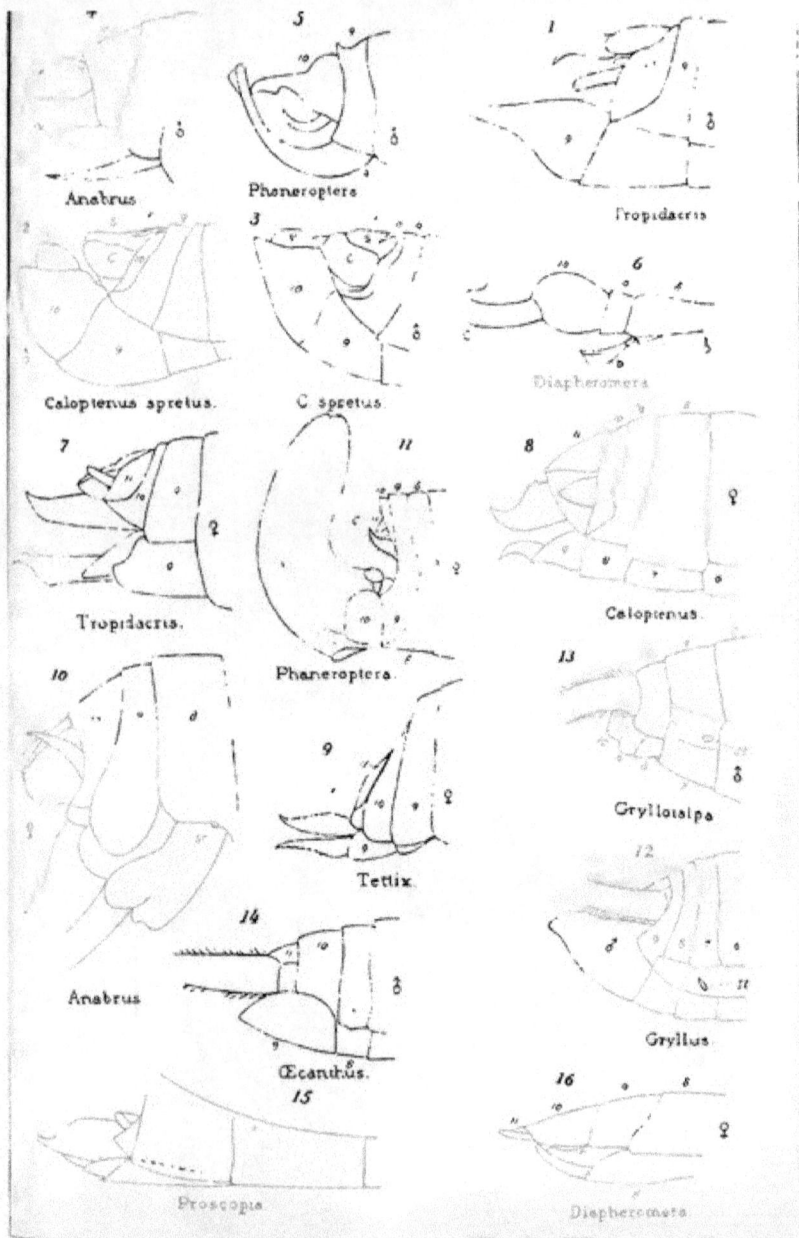

Anabrus

Phaneroptera

Tropidacris

Caloptenus spretus.

C. spretus

Diapheromera

Tropidacris.

Phaneroptera.

Caloptenus.

Anabrus

Tettix.

Gryllotalpa

Œcanthus.

Gryllus

Proscopia

Diapheromera

ORTHOPTERA. END OF ABDOMEN SIDE VIEW.

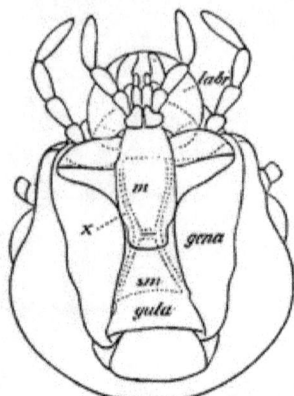

No. 1

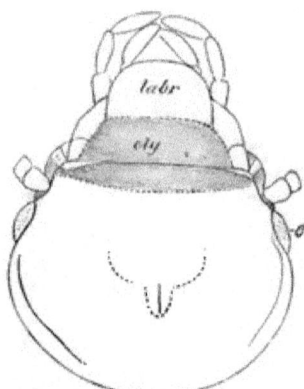

No. 2.

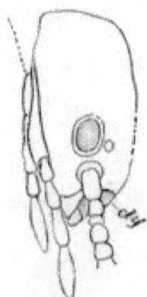

No. 5.

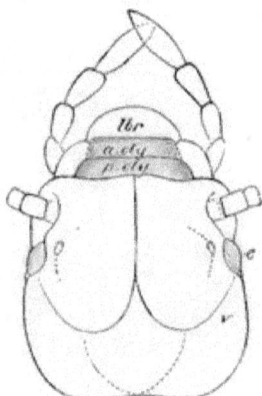

No. 4.

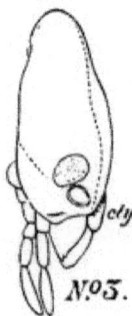

No. 3.

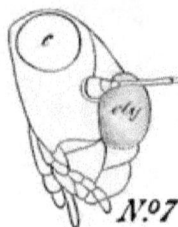

No. 7

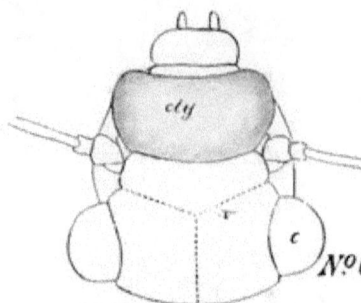

No. 6.

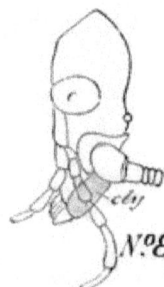

No. 8.

1-3. TERMOPSIS,   4, 5. TERMES,   6, 7. PSOCUS,   8. PTERONARCYS.

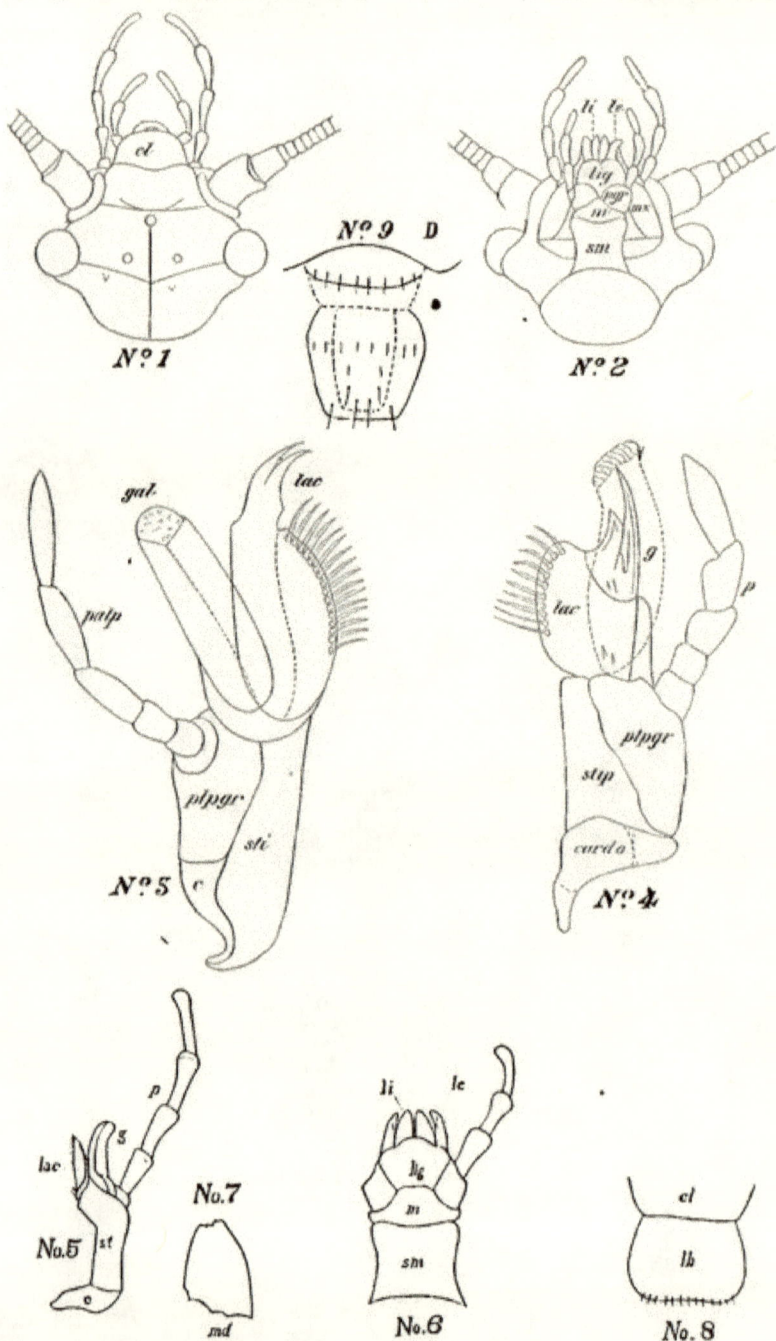

cl

№ 1

№ 9 D

*li le
lig
pgr
m   mx
sm*

№ 2

*gal   lac
palp
plpgr
sti
c*

№ 5

*g
lac   p
plpgr
stip
carda*

№ 4

*p
g
lac
st
c*

No. 5

No. 7

md

*li   le
lg
m
sm*

No. 6

*cl
lb*

No. 8

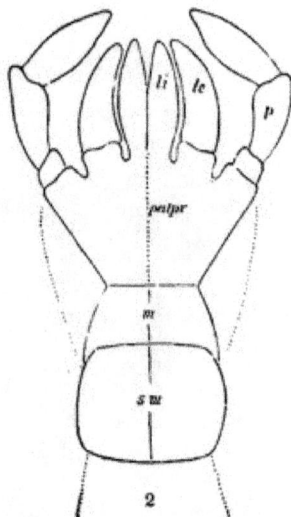

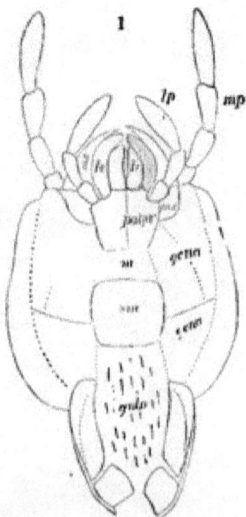
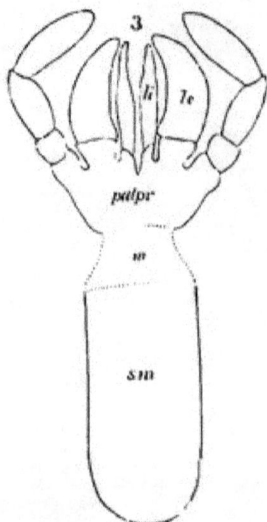

1, 2, 4, 5. TERMES.   3, 6-10. TERMOPSIS.

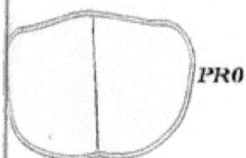

N.º 1.

PRO

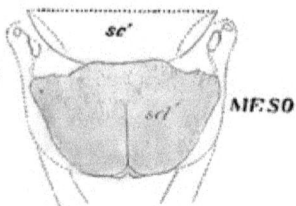

N.º 2.

sc'

scl

MESO

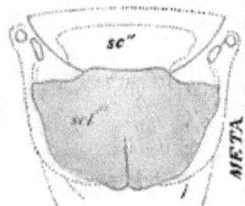

N.º 3.

sc"

scl"

META

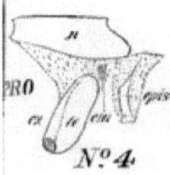

N.º 4.

PRO

cx   te   en   epis

N.º 6.

MET'

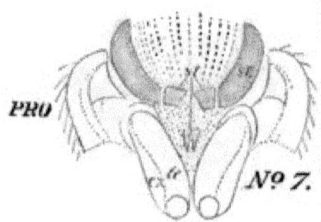

N.º 7.

PRO

Cx

MESO

post

epis

N.º 5.

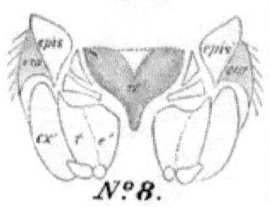

N.º 8.

epis

cx

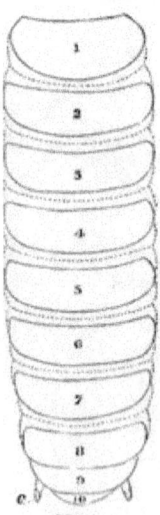

N.º 10.

1
2
3
4
5
6
7
8
9
10

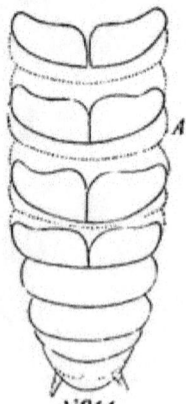

N.º 11.

A

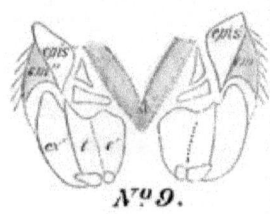

N.º 9.

epis

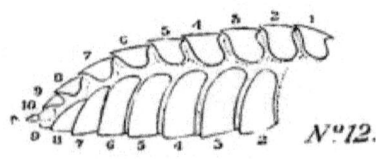

N.º 12.

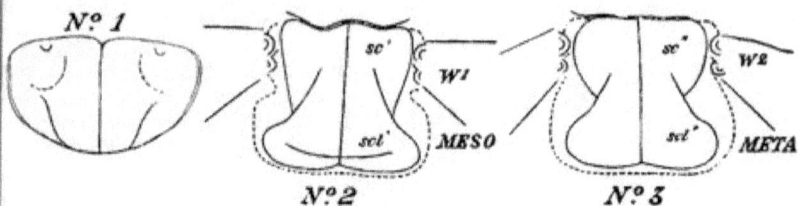

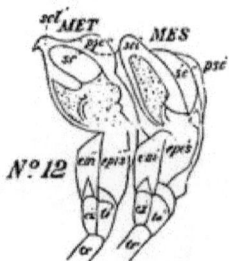

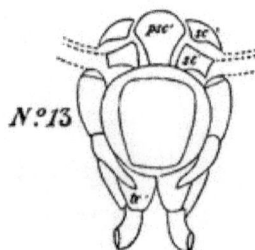

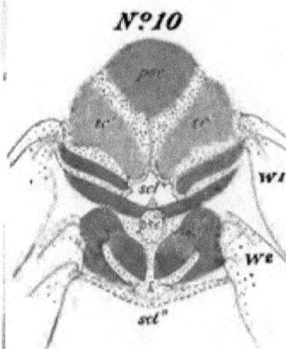

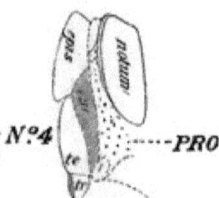

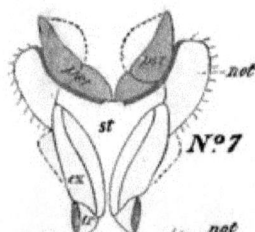

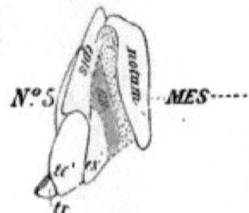

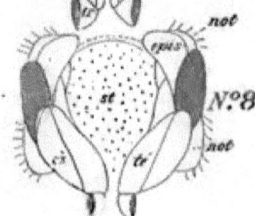

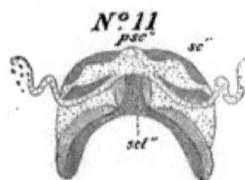

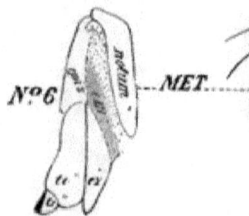

1-9. Termopsis.

10-14. Psocus.

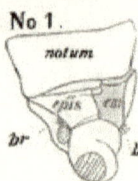

No 1.

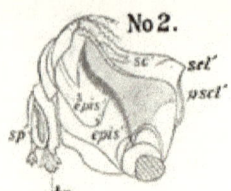

No 2.

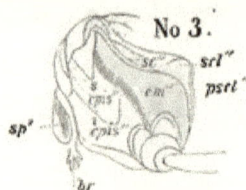

No 3.

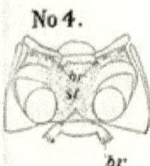

No 4.

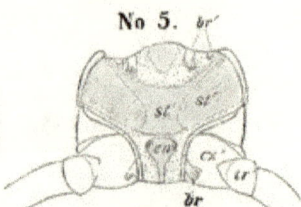

No 5.

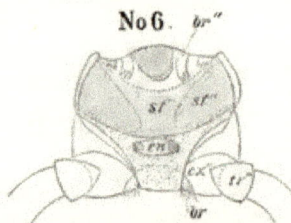

No 6.

PRO.   MES.   MET.

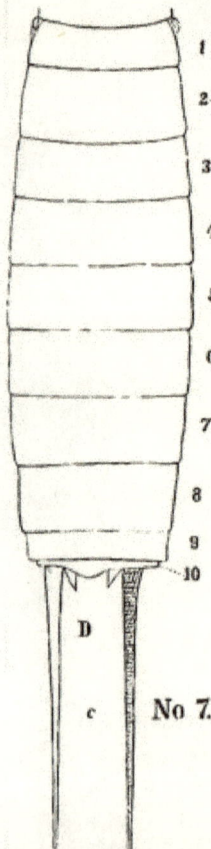

No 7.

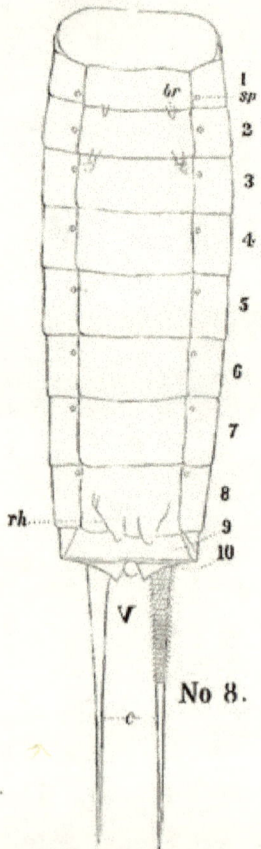

No 8.

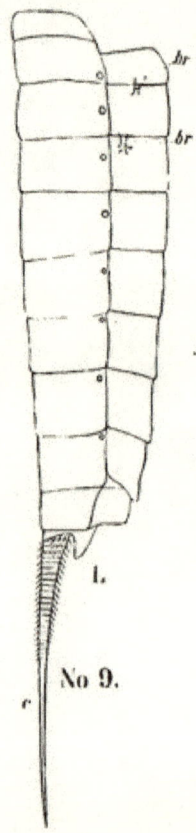

No 9.

Plate **XLV.**

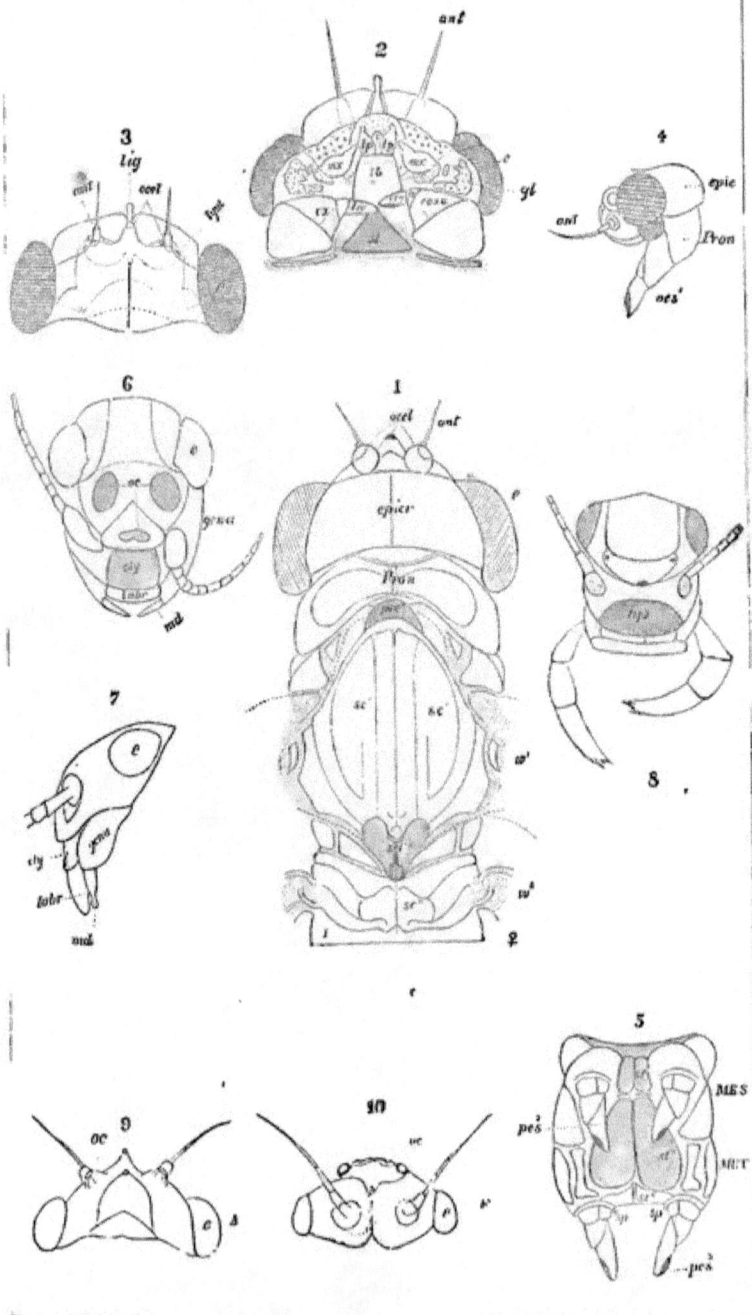

EPHEMERA.

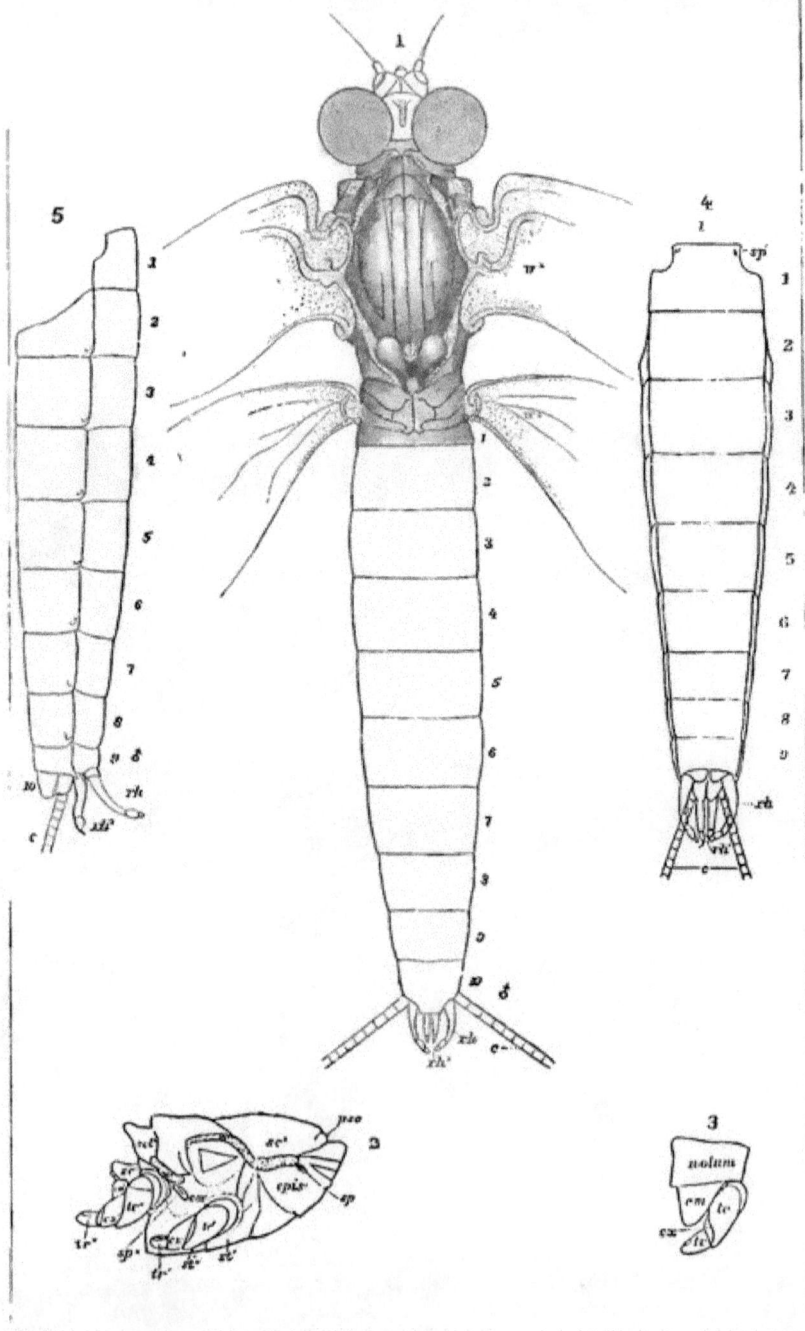

EPHEMERA.

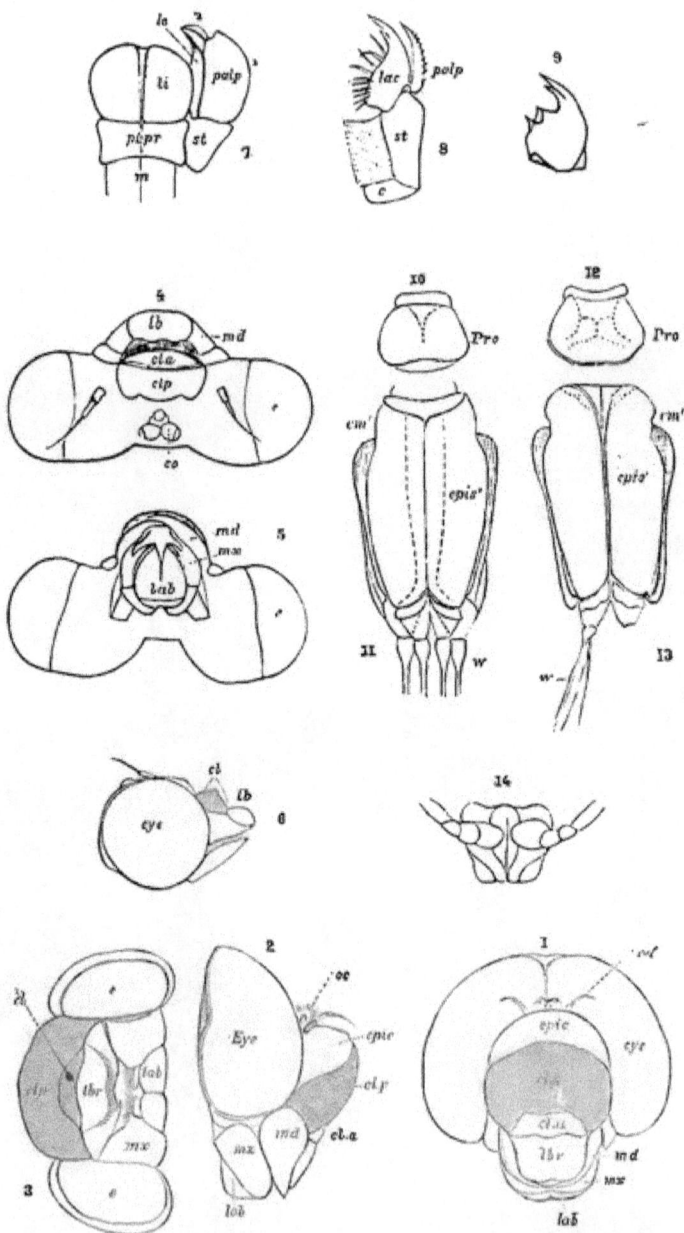

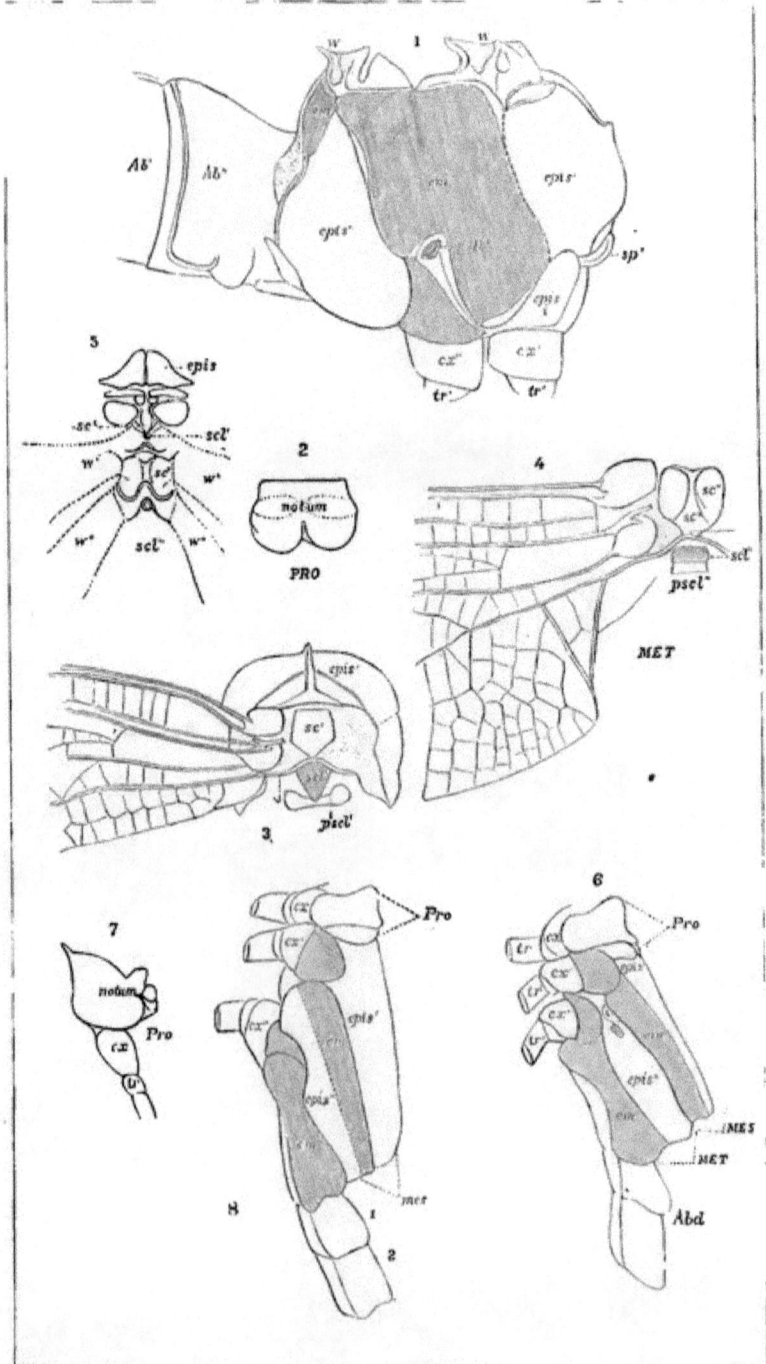

1-4 ÆSCHNA.   5, 6 CALOPTERYX.   7, 8 AGRION.

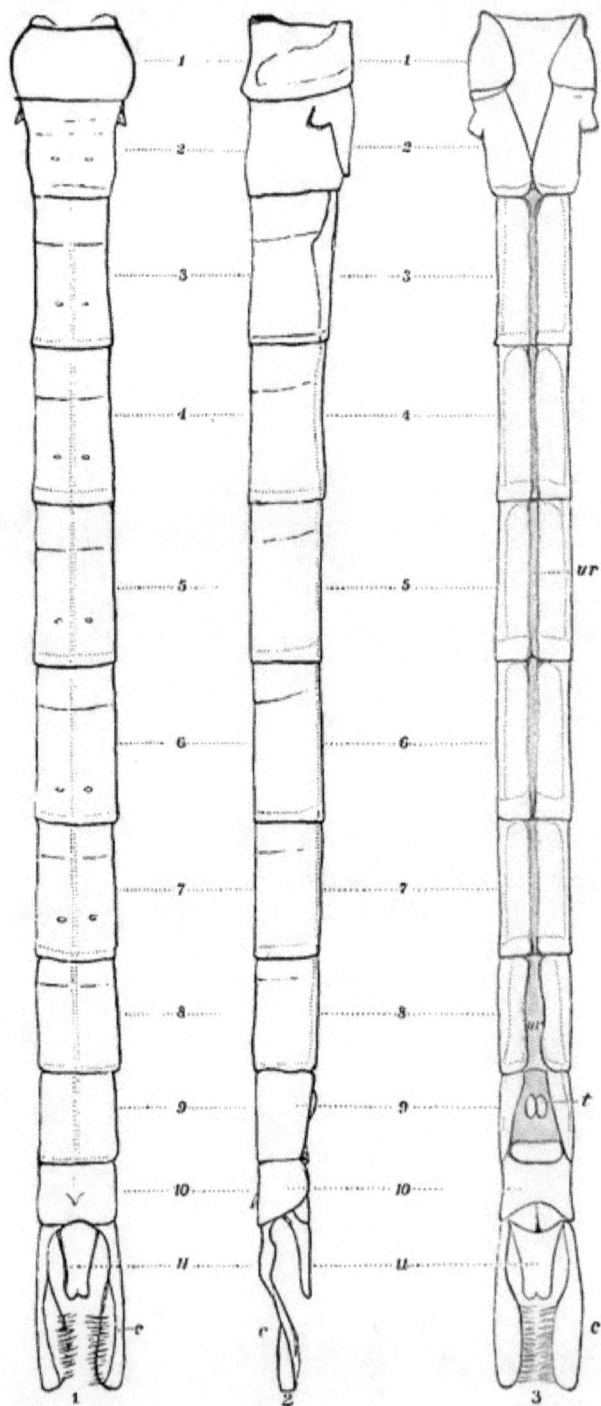

ABDOMEN OF ÆSCHNA HEROS.

Plate L.

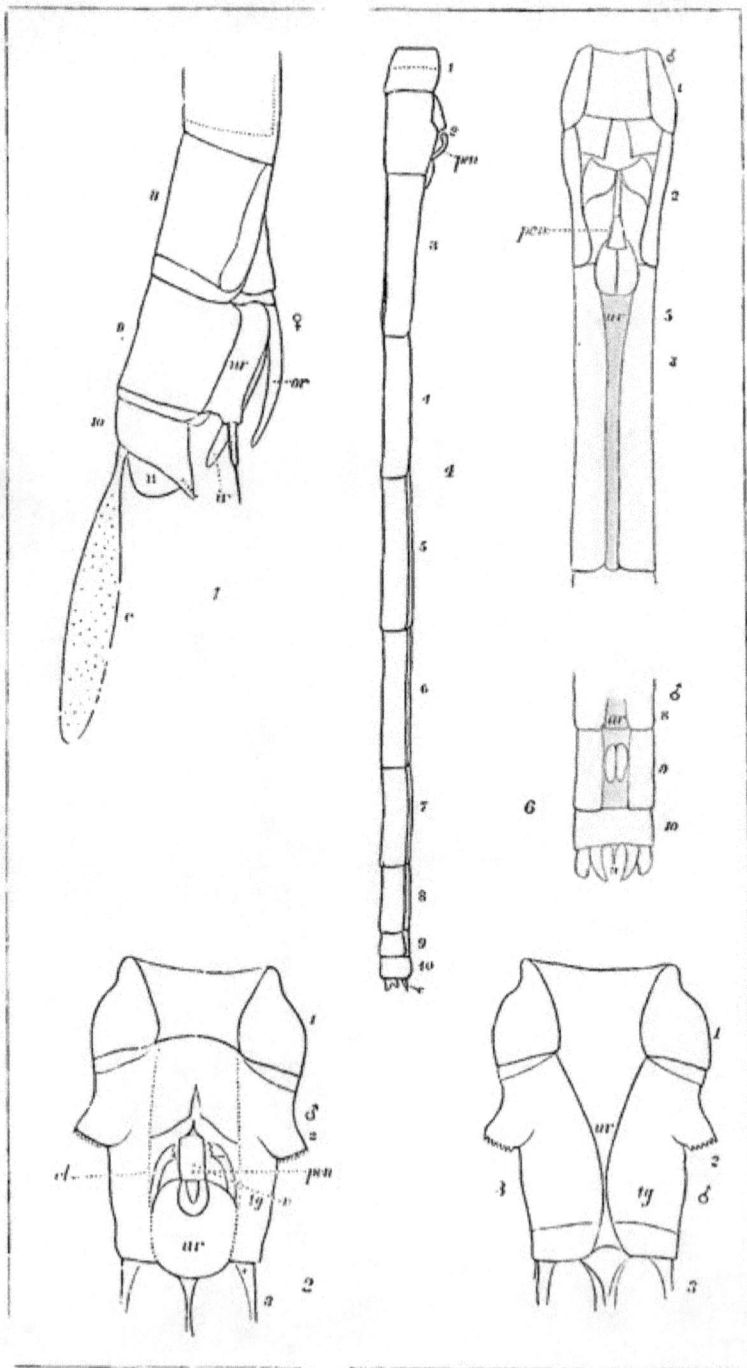

1-3. ÆSCHNA. 4-6. AGRION.

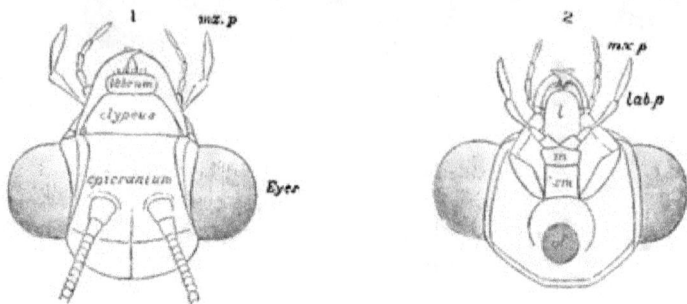

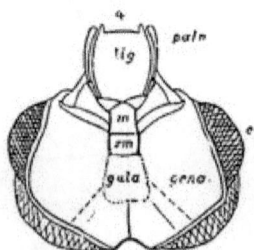

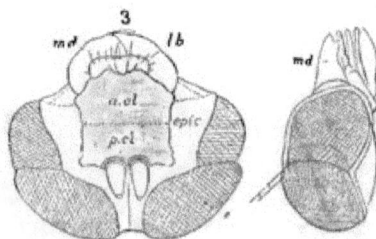

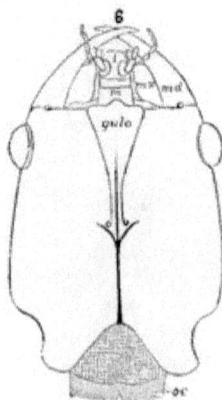

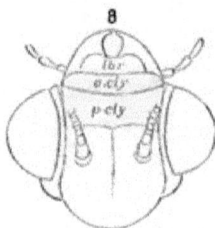

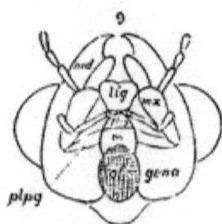

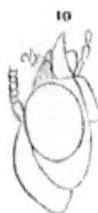

1, 2. MYRMELEON.   3, 4. ASCALAPHUS.   5-7. RAPHIDIA.   8-10. POLYSTŒCHOTES.

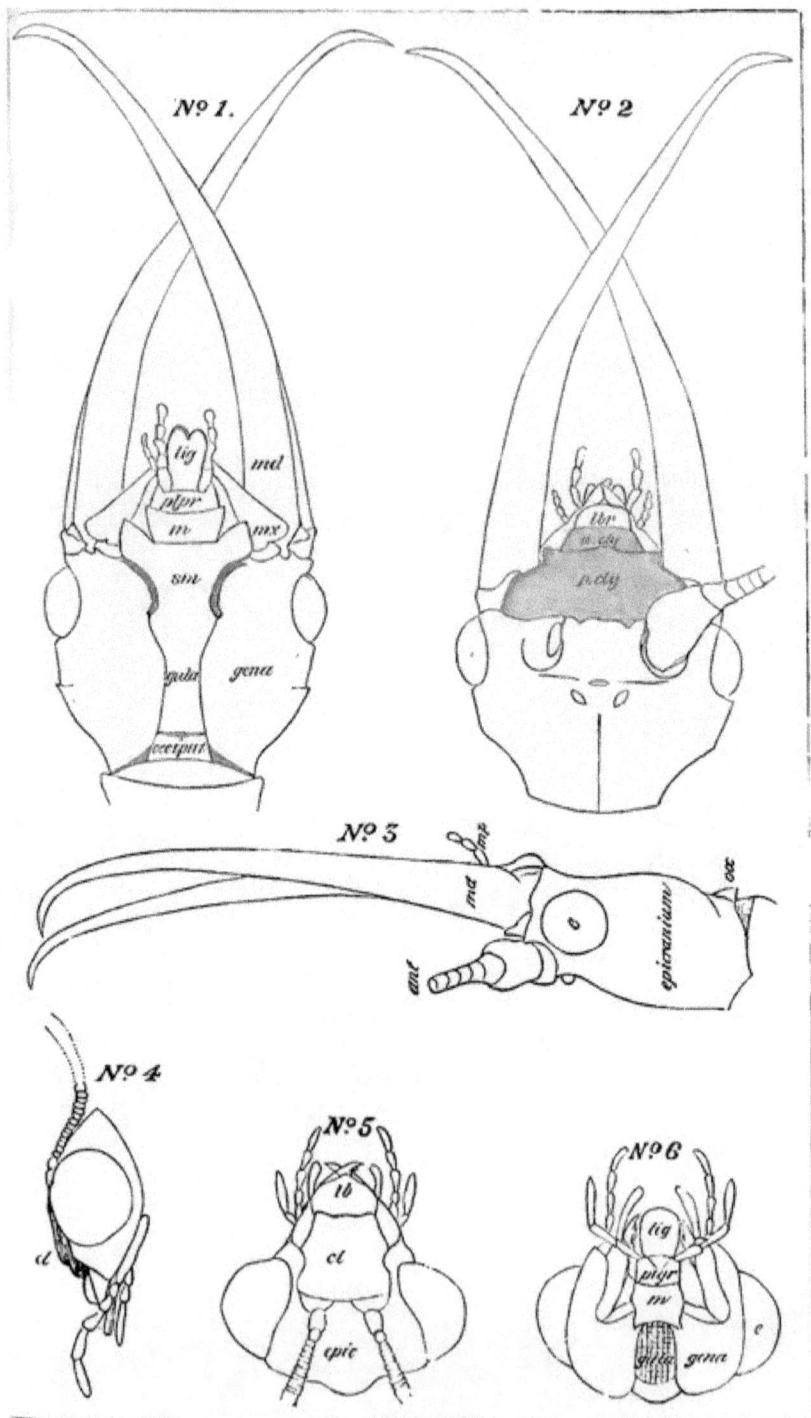

No 1.

No 2.

No 3

No 4

No 5

No 6

1-3. Corydalus.

4-6. Mantispa

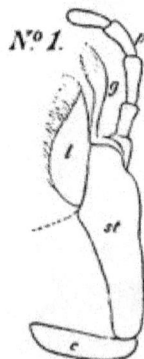

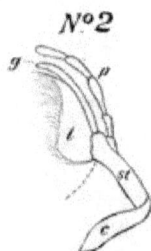

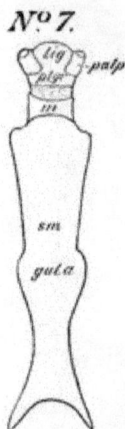

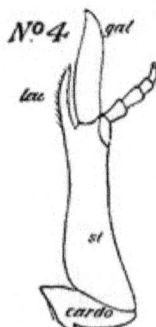

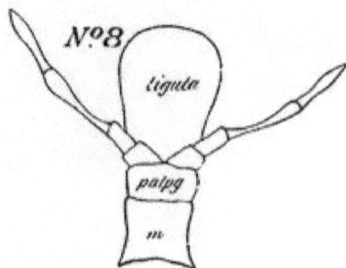

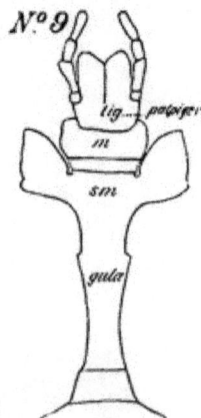

1, 5. MANTISPA.   2, 6. ASCALAPHUS.   3, 8. MYRMELEON.   4, 9. CORYDALUS.   7. RAPHIDIA.

Plate LIV.

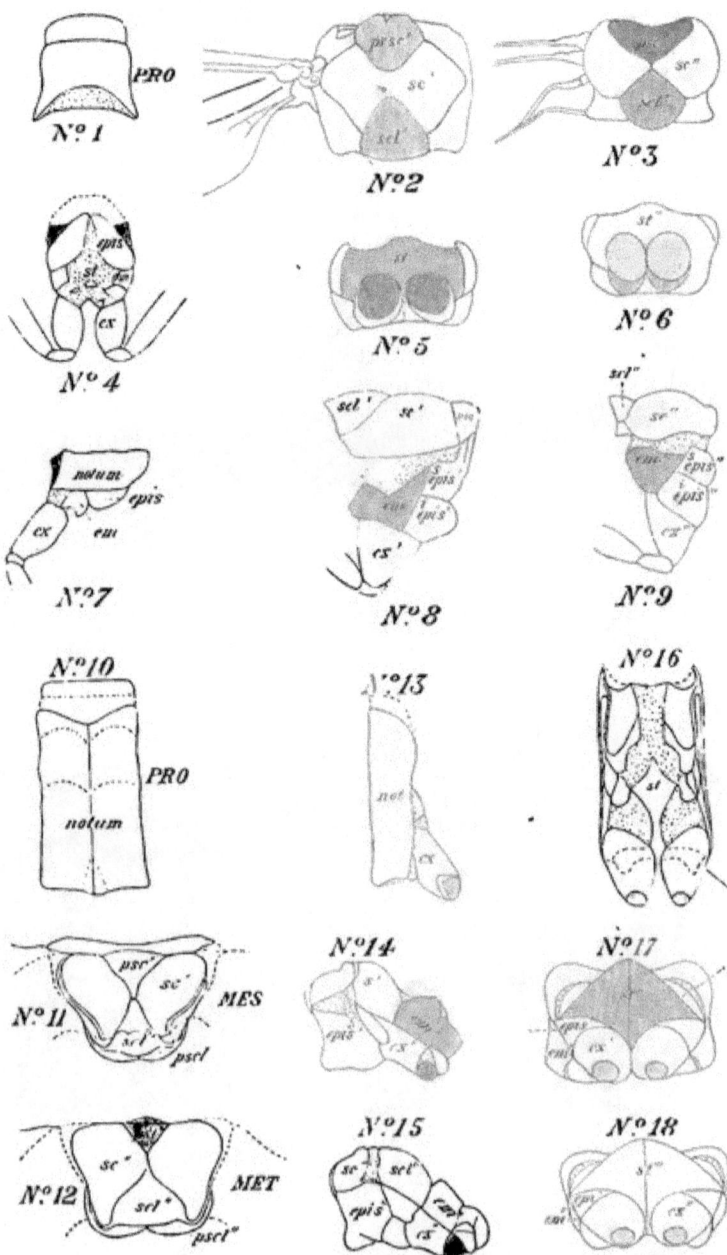

1-9. MYRMELEON.   10-18. RAPHIDIA.

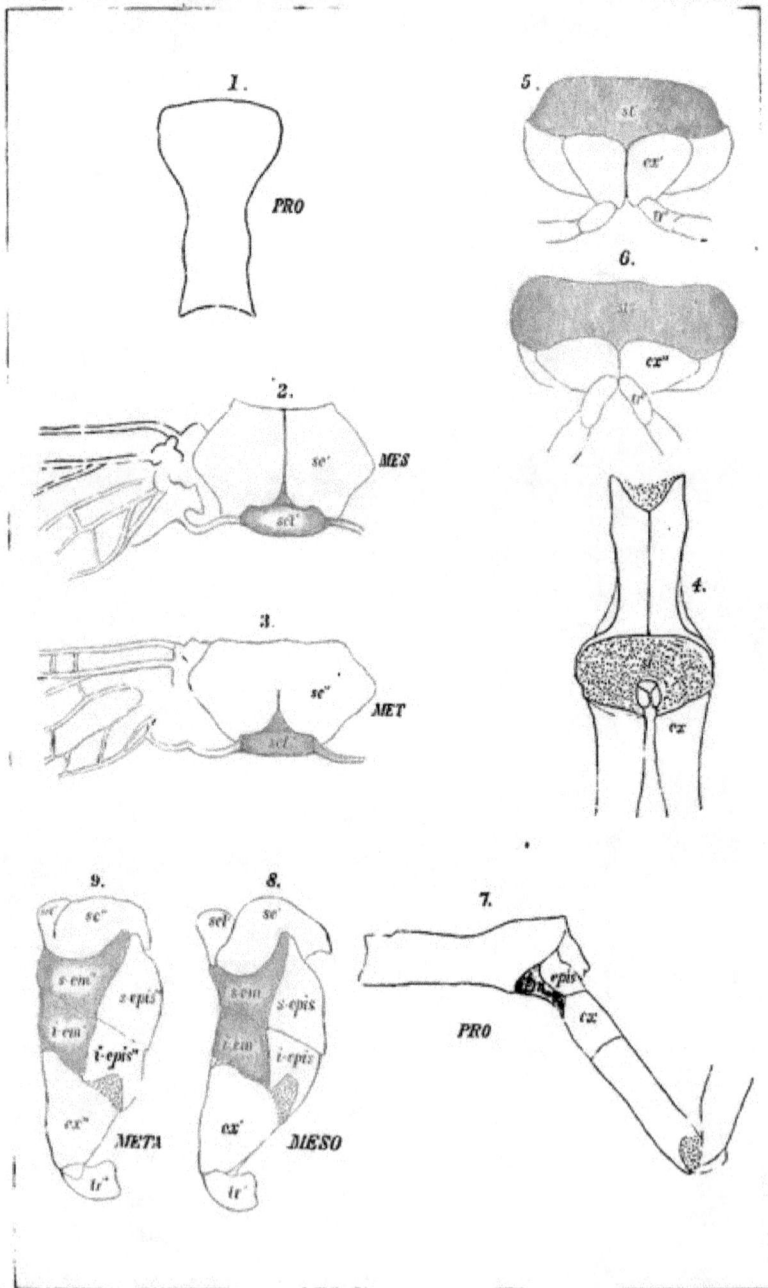

MANTISPA BRUNNEA.

Plate LVI.

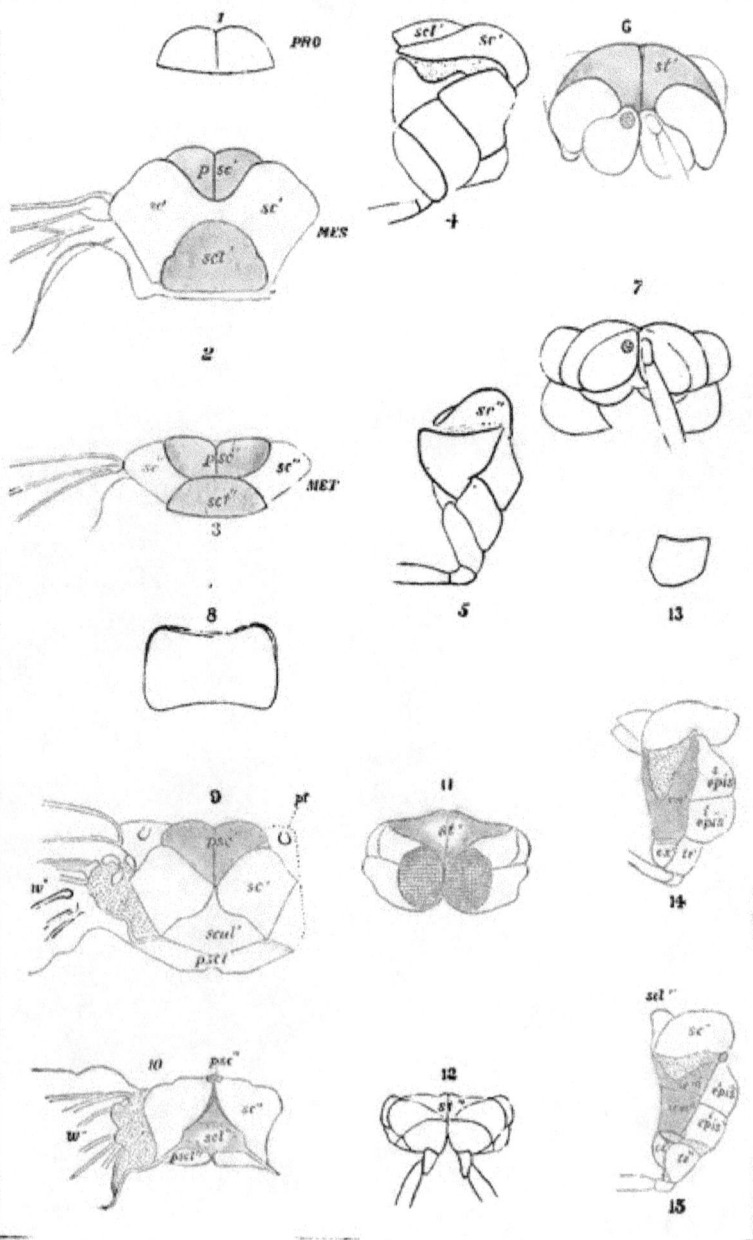

1-7. THORAX OF ASCALAPHUS.   8-15. POLYSTOECHOTES.

Plate LVII.

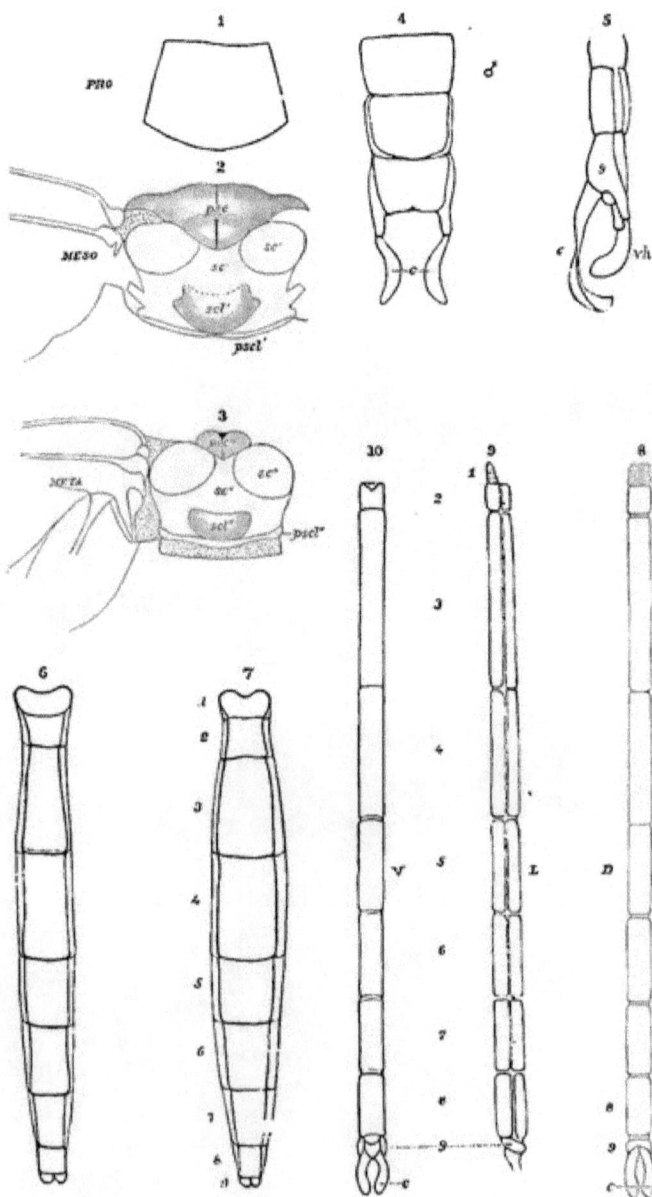

1-3. PTERONARCYS.   4, 5. CORYDALUS.   6, 7. ASCALAPHUS.   8-10. MYRMELEON.

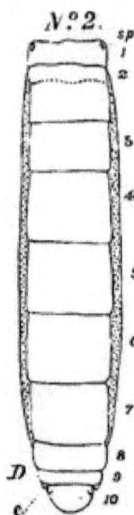

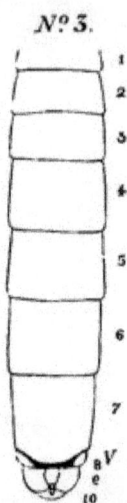

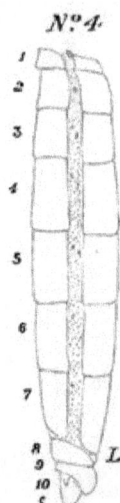

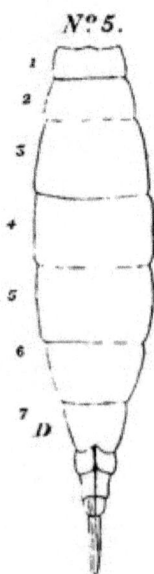

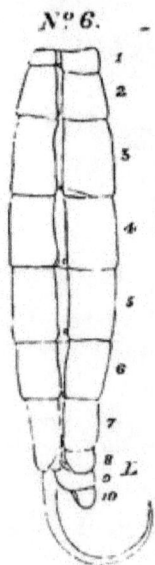

No. 2. No. 3. No. 4.

No. 5. No. 6. No. 7.

1. CORYDALIS.   2-4. POLYSTŒCHOTES.   5-7. RAPHIDIA.

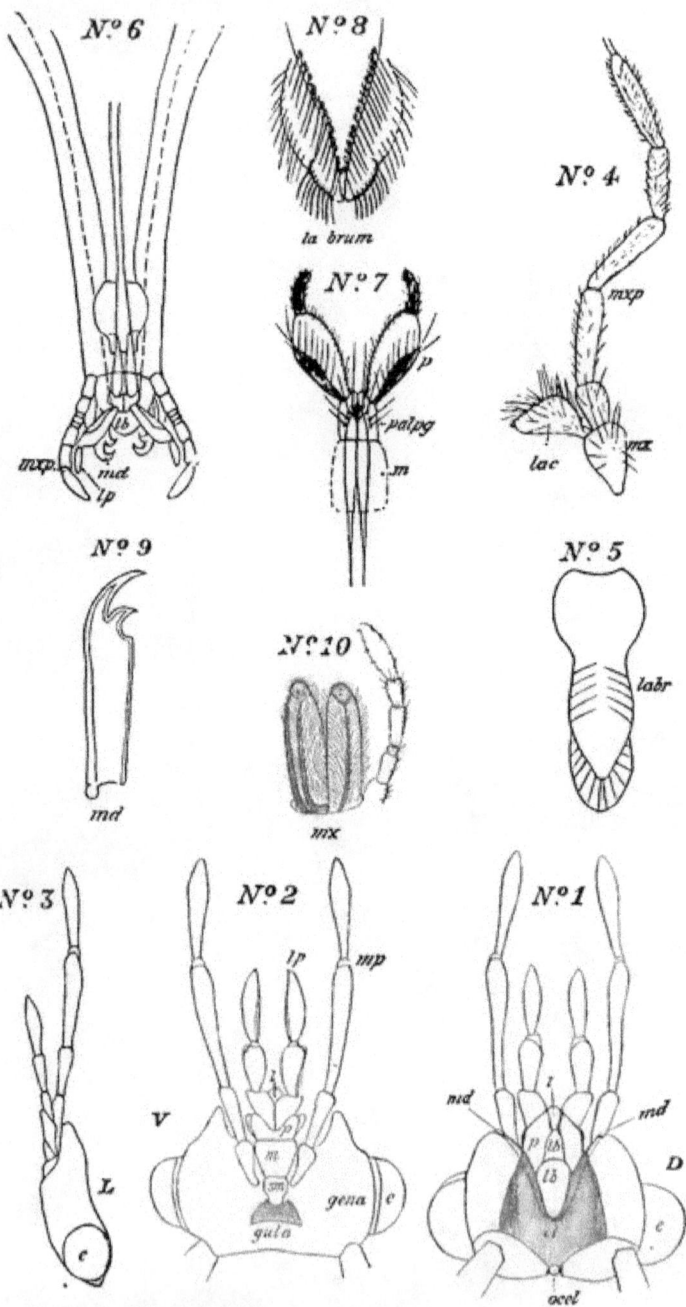

Plate LX.

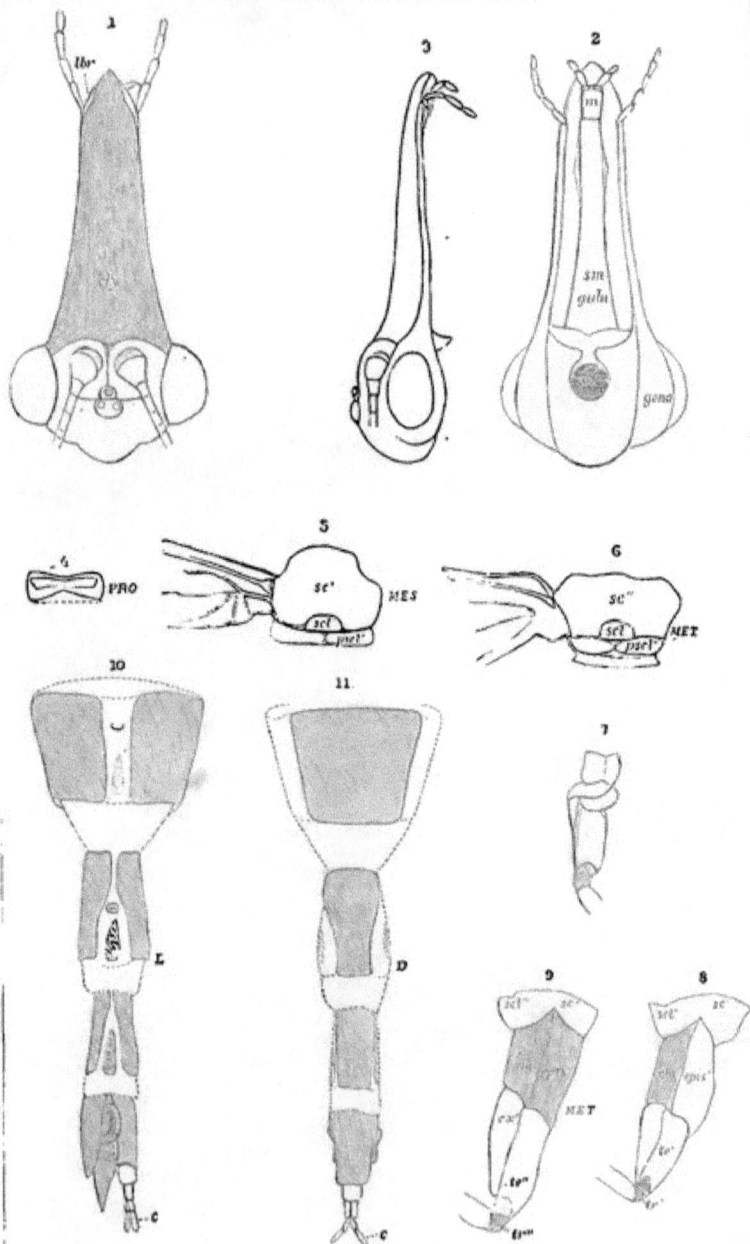

PANORPA.

No 4.
PRO

No 5.
MES

No 6.
MET

PRO
No 1.

MES
No 2.

No 7.

MET
No 3.

No 8.

D

V
No 9.

LIMNEPHILUS PUBES.

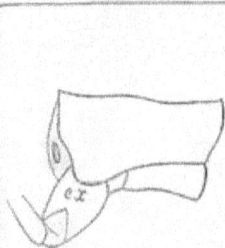

N.º 1.

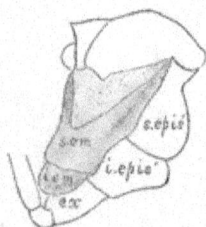

N.º 2.

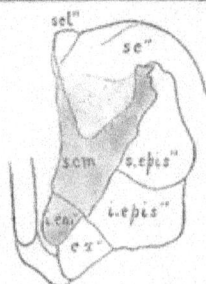

N.º 3.

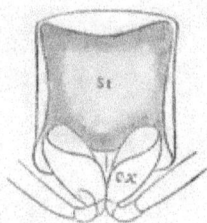

N.º 4.

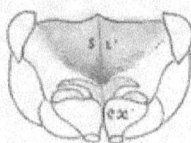

N.º 5.

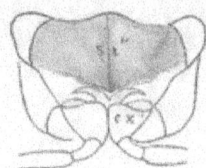

N.º 6.

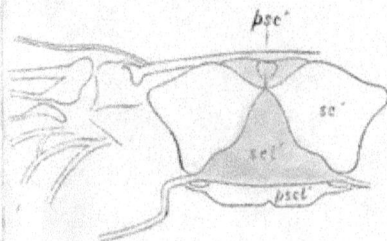

N.º 7.

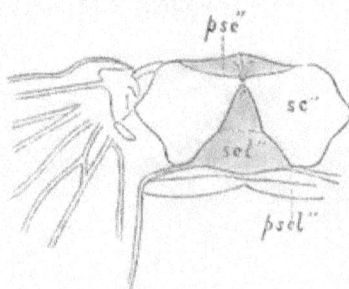

N.º 8.

THORAX OF CORYDALUS.

www.ingramcontent.com/pod-product-compliance
Lightning Source LLC
Chambersburg PA
CBHW030555270326
41927CB00007B/928